# SOCIAL INSECURITY

# SOCIAL INSECURITY

## THE CRISIS IN AMERICA'S SOCIAL SECURITY SYSTEM AND HOW TO PLAN NOW FOR YOUR OWN FINANCIAL SURVIVAL

Dorcas R. Hardy
**Former Commissioner of Social Security**

C. Colburn Hardy

VILLARD BOOKS   NEW YORK   1991

A Stonesong Press Book

A Stonesong Press book

Villard Books is a registered trademark of Random House, Inc.

Library of Congress Cataloging-in-Publication Data
Hardy, Dorcas R.
Social insecurity: the crisis in America's social security system and how to plan now
for your own financial survival/Dorcas R. Hardy and C. Colburn Hardy.— 1st ed.
p.      cm.
Includes index.
ISBN 0-679-40290-X
1. Social security—United States.   I. Hardy, C. Colburn.   II. Title.
HD7125.H33   1992        368.4'3'00973—dc20          91-50062

Manufactured in the United States of America

9  8  7  6  5  4  3  2

Book design by Richard Oriolo

First Edition

To the millions of working Americans
who are currently paying into Social Security,
a once well-intentioned system that
has become outmoded

# PREFACE

··················

**W**riting *Social Insecurity* was not easy but it was rewarding. It involved two individuals, living some 975 miles apart, with two different writing styles and two unique viewpoints: one based largely on the past and the other keyed to the future. We also have two financial frames of reference: the father astounded at the munificence of Social Security—with self and still-working wife, some $24,000 a year—not far from the highest annual benefits; the daughter facing a personal income tax of more than the same sum.

As we wrote this book, it soon became apparent that there was a significant dichotomy in our definitions of wealth. To the senior Hardy, who lived through the Great Depression and felt lucky when he was paid $100 per month, working affluence was $30,000 a year. This means that, by formula, a financially secure retirement was 70 percent of that compensation, or $21,000—roughly $11,000 from Social Security and $10,000 from pensions and investments. By age seventy-five, with inflation, those figures had to be adjusted by about 33 percent to $40,000 income.

To the former-commissioner daughter, whose highest federal

pay was just under $90,000, working affluence was a *minimum* of $125,000 a year, with retirement finances providing nearly that sum in the 2020s . . . a far smaller portion from Social Security and vastly more from personal savings.

These different viewpoints are significant today but will be even more so "tomorrow." On what now appear to be valid projections, the actual dollars paid by Social Security will continue to soar even as the buying power of those payments decreases. To retire comfortably, the average individual must have minimum private savings of $250,000 today; $500,000 when quitting in the early years of the next century; and $1 million for those who stop work around 2020.

Keep those figures in mind when you calculate your financial future. What appeared to be a welcome annual sum fifty years ago is now less than what you may be paying in taxes. In another half century, income of $1,000 *a week* will be equivalent to $1,000 per *month* today. To paraphrase Senator Everett Dirksen, "A million here and a million there and the first thing you know, you're talking about real money."

America's Social Security system will be in serious trouble soon after the start of the twenty-first century. This is not a pleasant prospect. Many people who should know better scoff at this prediction, but it is inevitable unless major changes are made soon.

Fortunately there are signs that leaders in the academic, business, and political fields are beginning to recognize the seriousness of this situation and to advance proposals that can ease, and, we hope, solve the pending crisis.

Because Social Security is a federal program, Congress can, and should, take leadership but, as is stressed throughout this book, the primary responsibility for building retirement income by direct savings and through pension plans must be with the individual.

As Social Security taxes continue to escalate, there are increasing signs of concern, both in Congress and among the public. The more people know about the Social Security system, the more apprehensive they will be. One of the purposes of this book is to provide readers with the information they need to be able to contribute to the upcoming debates on the subject and to start building their own retirement assets.

We are confident that improvements will be made. Retirement financing, dating back only a relatively short fifty-five years, has made a significant start with: (a) pension plans that require contributions, directly and/or through employers; (b) greater reliance on personal savings; and (c) the magic of compounding with investments.

Once a national retirement policy is established, Social Security will again become the base, not the major source, of retirement income and will be supplemented by greatly increased personal savings.

*Social Insecurity* won't solve all the problems of financing retirement but it can help to explain the issues and, we hope, will lead to the enactment of some much-needed measures. There is still time to make Social Security work better, to ensure its stability, and to work toward a financially secure retirement for almost all Americans.

Both of us have been sufficiently involved in government and community service to be aware of how Social Insecurity developed, why Congress has been so slow to recognize the coming crisis, and what steps will be needed to initiate and carry out essential changes. We are realistic optimists and are confident that, once political and business leaders understand the potential severity of the pending crisis, there will be constructive action and a start toward our recommended goals.

This book is written in two parts: the first by Dorcas R. Hardy, who served as U.S. Commissioner of Social Security under presidents Reagan and Bush after serving as assistant secretary of Health and Human Services, where she supervised programs for the elderly. Part I summarizes the history of Social Security, explains present programs and benefits, and outlines what's wrong now and the severe dangers in the near future. One of the major recommendations is that, for their retirement income, individuals must rely less on Social Security and more on personal, private savings.

Part II shows the reader how to attain such goals. It is written by Dorcas's father, C. Colburn Hardy. He is the author of twenty-six books on investments, personal money management, pension plans, and retirement planning. His counsel reflects experience as a director of a multibillion-dollar international money management firm and as an active member of the Florida Pepper Commission on Aging.

We think this book will be of great interest to anyone who plans to be alive in the next century—nine years from now. If you have already retired, it will help you to understand the debate over Social Security that seems certain to grow in the coming years. And even though the primary emphasis in Part II is on planning for retirement, you will find a number of techniques discussed there that can improve your money management even after you begin drawing a pension. If you have not yet retired, we hope Part I will disabuse you of your illusions about Social Security, and that Part II will provide a blueprint for retirement planning.

No book is written in a vacuum, and we would like to thank the many people who provided information and encouragement and took time to discuss their views. A special note of appreciation goes to the employees of the Social Security Administration, to government officials, and to members of the U.S. Congress and their staff.

Finally, credit goes to Ruth E. Hardy, mother, wife, confidante, and critic. She was patient, questioning, and ever ready to remind us that we were writing a book that should be interesting, informative, and constructive. We have tried to take her advice and we hope that you, the reader, will feel that we have succeeded.

# CONTENTS

......................

## Part II: Planning for Your Retirement

# INTRODUCTION

. . . . . . . . . . . . . . . . .

# THE MESS WE ARE IN

We ought to call it Social Insecurity, not Social Security. The Social Security system is a ticking time bomb. In the next century, just a few years away, the United States will face a potentially devastating crisis: the retirement checks that should be sent to benefit millions of Americans will *not* be there. This crisis will not affect those now receiving Social Security, but to maintain benefits for future retirees, significant changes must be made by Congress. Reform will not be easy.

Imagine walking into your congressman's office with irrefutable evidence that the United States in the next century will face a possibly ruinous economic and social crisis. You assure your representative, however, that opportunities exist to take early corrective action to head off this impending disaster. Your optimism that such action will occur is dampened when you tell your congressman what issues are involved. Social Security? Forget it. The senior citizen organizations won't allow Congress even to discuss the issue. The federal deficit? It's a no-win topic. Private pension policy? It's boring, a non-vote-getter. Because of its politically unappealing nature, the most critical economic issue America will face in the twenty-first century continues to simmer unabated.

The hard demographic and financial facts are that future retirees are unlikely, under any circumstances, to benefit as much from Social Security as their parents have.

The pending crisis stems from numerous factors: the current birth dearth that followed the postwar baby boom; ever-rising Social Security benefits; a lack of integrity in governmental policy making, which has perpetrated the myth that huge "trust" funds back promised benefits; the pressures to use Social Security assets to pay for other types of social services; and the simple fact that people are living longer. The bottom line is that there are going to be many more older people, and relatively fewer working people to support them. By 2030, there will be only two workers for every retiree compared to three workers for every retiree today.

This ratio is crucial because Social Security is a pay-as-you-go system. Current taxes pay for current benefits. If benefits for future retirees are to remain unchanged, some project that payroll taxes may have to go as high as 40 percent.

Despite window dressing, Social Security is not a funded pension system where workers' money is invested and then paid back, with interest, later. It is a straightforward transfer of wealth from workers to retirees.

For more than fifty years, Social Security has provided the solid base for retirement income, and today pays out over $750 million per day ($275 billion per year)—representing more than 20 percent of the federal budget!

As a practical matter, it is unlikely that the Social Security system will collapse completely, the way some private pension systems have. More likely the fallout will be a combination of reduced benefits for retirees and increased taxes for everyone.

Fortunately, in the United States, the private sector usually develops effective alternatives, and retirement income should be no exception. The individual must assume greater responsibility for his or her own after-work income by personal savings directly and through pension plans, sometimes with support from the employer.

There are also actions Congress can take to minimize the potential damage. It can begin with realistic, balanced retirement policies that encourage private savings by individuals. A start should be to restore the full tax deductibility of Individual Retirement Accounts, which was taken away in the 1986 tax reform.

Other important measures should be to: (1) raise the limits of annual contributions to all types of pension programs; (2) revise the mandated withdrawal schedule now for the actuarial lives of the recipients, to permit beneficiaries of pension plans to meet the realities of a longer life span; and (3) privatize a portion of Social Security taxes so that the individual worker can be responsible for financing his or her own retirement.

All these actions would be very helpful, but the ultimate responsibility for retirement income is *yours.* If you plan to rely heavily on Social Security, as the average retiree now does, your golden years are going to be a time of want and financial anxiety. What you save, or fail to save, while working, will determine what you can, or cannot do, upon retirement. A program of serious and consistent savings, and wise investment, begun *now* will assure a financially secure retirement.

# SOME
# DEFINITIONS

..............................

Social Security is a national program of the federal government supported by nearly every worker in America. It pays benefits to forty million people, primarily retired workers. Like any program of the federal government, it has its own private language consisting of acronyms, liberally seasoned with jargon. Here are a few of the more important terms, together with explanations.

**COLA:** Cost of Living Adjustment. This is an annual increase in Social Security benefits based on the previous year's increase in the Consumer Price Index (the year used runs from October to October). Before 1972, Congress enacted several benefit increases designed to keep benefit amounts in line with inflation. In 1972, Congress passed legislation providing for automatic adjustments, or COLAs. COLA increases started in 1975. In recent years COLA increases have been in the range of 3 to 5 percent. In the late 1970s they were over 10 percent.

**DI:** Disability Insurance. When first enacted in 1956, the program was limited to persons aged fifty and over. In 1961 this age limitation was removed. DI is funded through the FICA payroll tax. To qualify for benefits, the applicant must demonstrate a long-term physical or mental incapacity for any "substantial gainful activity."

**Early Retirement:** Approximately 70 percent of all workers retire before the normal retirement age of sixty-five. Congress first authorized early retirement for women in 1956; men were authorized to retire early in 1961. At the earliest permitted retirement age—sixty-two—beneficiaries receive payments 20 percent lower than they would have received if they had retired at sixty-five. For retirement between sixty-two and sixty-five, benefits increase on a sliding scale.

**Earnings Test:** The penalty for continuing to earn income while receiving a Social Security check. You can make approximately $10,000 without any penalty, but if you earn more than that amount, the benefits you receive from Social Security are reduced. The earnings test applies only to earned income, not to investment income, and only to people under the age of seventy. From seventy on, you can make as much money as you want and still collect full Social Security benefits. Proposals to eliminate the earnings test are pending in Congress.

**FICA:** The four letters on your payroll stub stand for the Federal Insurance Contributions Act. The FICA tax is really three taxes that, on paper at least, go into three separate trust funds. At present Old-Age and Survivors Insurance receives 5.60 percent, Disability Insurance receives 0.60 percent, and Health Insurance receives 1.45 percent of the payroll deduction, which totals 7.65 percent. The employer pays an equal amount, for a total of 15.3 percent of salary up to $53,400. (The wage base for Health Insurance is $125,000, with employee and employer each contributing 1.45 percent up to that ceiling.)

**HCFA:** The Health Care Financing Administration. This organization oversees the administration of the Medicare and Medicaid programs. It is a part of the Department of Health and Human Services and has its headquarters in Washington, D.C.

**HI:** Hospital Insurance, which is Part A of Medicare. It is funded through the FICA payroll tax. The funds are administered by the Health Care Financing Administration.

**Medicaid** is a means-tested health-care program for the needy. Established in 1965, it is jointly financed by the federal and state governments. It is administered by the states, which set their own income-eligibility standards. The major expenditure for seniors is for nursing home care.

**Medicare:** The federal health insurance program primarily for individuals over age sixty-five that was enacted in 1965. It consists of two parts. Part A, or HI, covers Hospital costs. Part B, or SMI, covers doctors' fees and other nonhospital costs.

**Normal Retirement Age:** From 1935 to the present, the normal retirement age has been sixty-five. In the year 2000, gradual increases in the normal retirement age will begin; it will reach age sixty-six by 2009 and sixty-seven by 2027. Early retirement at sixty-two will continue to be an option. However, the percentage reduction in early retirement benefits will increase as the normal retirement age increases.

**OASDI:** Old-Age, Survivors, and Disability Insurance. The two trust funds Old-Age and Survivors Insurance (OASI) and Disability Insurance (DI) are often combined for reporting purposes, producing the acronym OASDI. Less commonly Health Insurance (HI) is also added, creating OASDHI.

**PIA:** Primary Insurance Amount. This is the dollar benefit, based on a worker's earnings history, that is paid to an individual who claims benefits at the normal retirement age. It is also the base for disability and survivor benefits. Early retirement payments are lower.

**SECA:** The Self-Employed Contributions Act. SECA is FICA for the self-employed. People who work for themselves pay a tax equal to the sum of an employer's and an employee's contributions under FICA. However, half of the amount is deductible for income tax purposes.

**SMI:** Supplementary Medical Insurance. This is Part B of the Medicare program and covers doctors' fees and other nonhospital costs. Approximately one-quarter of the cost of this program is funded by deductions from participants' Social Security checks. The remaining three-quarters comes from the general revenues of the federal government. SMI funds are administered by the Health Care Financing Agency.

**Spousal Benefits:** A spouse who did not work outside the home qualifies for a benefit equaling approximately 50 percent of the benefit paid to the retired worker, giving the couple approximately 150 percent of the income that the retired worker would receive if he (or she) were single.

**SSA:** Social Security Administration. The federal agency that administers the Social Security system. It is a part of the Department of Health and Human Services and employs more than 63,000 people, who process and maintain wage records for all workers in America and send out half a billion benefit checks annually. The headquarters are in Baltimore, Maryland; there are more than 1,300 branch offices worldwide. SSA operates the world's largest civilian telephone network; the toll-free number is 1-800-234-5772.

**SSI:** Supplementary Security Income. Enacted by Congress in 1972 to replace federal and state programs for the needy elderly, blind, and disabled. The SSI program is administered by the Social Security Administration.

**Taxation of Social Security Benefits:** Before 1984, Social Security benefits were not subject to federal income tax. Since 1984 up to one half of the benefit may be subject to tax, if income from all sources exceeds specified amounts—$25,000 for an individual, $32,000 for a couple filing jointly. Income from all sources includes income from Social Security, earned income, and investment income. Because the threshold figures are not indexed for inflation, this tax will bite more and more retired people as the years go by.

# A FEW DATES TO
# REMEMBER

......................

**1935:** Social Security Act is signed by President Franklin D. Roosevelt, establishing a system of old-age benefits for workers in commerce and industry. The system is nationwide, federally administered, compulsory, and contributory. There is no provision allowing those with private pension coverage to opt out of the system. Social Security is to begin paying benefits in 1942.

**1939:** Following the recommendations of a blue-ribbon panel, Congress authorizes supplemental benefits for dependents of retired workers and for surviving dependents in case of death.

**1940:** First monthly benefit check is paid to Ida Mae Fuller of Ludlow, Vermont. The check is for $22.54.

**1950:** First tax increase. This increase had originally been scheduled for 1940; Congress postponed it several times. Congress also increases benefits by 77 percent and greatly expands the number of workers covered by the system.

**1956:** Congress initiates the disability insurance program, limiting its coverage to persons over the age of fifty. Women are allowed to take early retirement at age 62, with reduced benefits.

**1960:** The age limitation of fifty for disability payments is removed.

**1961:** Congress allows men to take early retirement at age sixty-two, with reduced benefits.

**1965:** After years of intense debate, Medicare is enacted. Hospitalization (Part A) is funded by an increase in Social Security taxes. Doctors' fees and other nonhospital costs (Part B) are partially funded by a deduction from the retired person's Social Security check; the rest of the money for Part B comes from the general revenues of the federal government. Also in this year, Congress establishes Medicaid, a medical assistance program for the poor.

**1972:** Congress, tired of enacting politically influenced benefit increases every few years, passes legislation providing for annual cost of living increases, or COLAs. The first COLA comes in 1975.

**1974:** The Supplemental Security Income program (SSI) replaces federal and state assistance programs for the needy elderly, blind, and disabled.

**1977:** With the Social Security system in deep financial trouble, Congress revises the benefit formula and increases taxes dramatically. These revisions are expected to put Social Security back onto a sound footing for the next fifty years.

**1980:** Congress reduces disability benefits.

**1981:** With Social Security again in financial trouble, President Ronald Reagan appoints a bipartisan National Commission on Social Security Reform.

**1983:** Acting on the commission's proposals, Congress makes a number of changes in the Social Security system. Beginning with 1983, the annual cost of living increase in benefits comes six months later in the year than had previously been the case. Previously scheduled payroll tax increases are accelerated, and taxes for the self-employed also go up. In addition, Congress provides for a gradual increase in the retirement age from sixty-five to sixty-seven, to commence after the year 2000, and, for the first time, taxes the benefits of retirees with relatively high incomes. The package is hailed as a "permanent" solution to the problems of Social Security.

**1988:** Congress enacts the Medicare Catastrophic Coverage Act, the first major revision of Medicare since its inception in 1965. The most important provision of the new law is full coverage for hospital stays, no matter how long they last. Under the old law, full coverage had been limited to the first sixty days of a hospital stay. Mindful of the budget deficit, Congress provides that the elderly will pay for their new benefits through an increase in monthly Medicare premiums and, for the well-to-do, a surcharge on income taxes.

**1989:** After massive protests by the elderly, Congress repeals the Medicare Catastrophic Coverage Act of 1988.

**1994:** Projections indicate that Medicare will be running a deficit by this year.

**2010:** Social Security is expected to start running a deficit no later than 2010.

# PART I

# What to Do About Social Security

# ONE

........

# HISTORY: HOW WE GOT INTO THIS MESS

The Social Security Act is one of the most important pieces of legislation ever passed by Congress. Its goals are admirable: to provide retirement, survivors, and disability benefits to workers and their families, and to assume some of the health care costs borne by the elderly and the long-term disabled.

## THE WHALE IN THE BATHTUB
...

Social Security is also the single largest financial entity in the federal government. Currently it receives more than $300 billion dollars each year, primarily from payroll taxes, and it pays benefits of about $275 billion to nearly forty million people.

At present, more than 95 percent of all working Americans pay into and are covered by Social Security. For most working people, Social Security taxes, paid half by the individual and half by the employer, are the largest federal levy on their income—as much as $10,247 a year.

# How Big Is
# Social Security? Very Big.
### ...

Just to put the massive expenditures of Social Security in perspective:

Benefit checks every year total $275 billion—and are growing.

This equates to:

$750 million per day, or
$32 million per hour, every day of the year, or
$8,700 per second.

Compare these expenditures with some items from the defense budget (this is a favorite Washington pastime):

- One F-15 tactical jet fighter costs $20 million. This is what Social Security spends in about 50 minutes.
- Removing one navy battleship from mothballs and getting it ready for service: $450 million, or about 18 hours of Social Security checks.
- One Patriot anti-missile missile: $1 million, or about 2 ½ minutes of Social Security payout.

And it will get bigger:

The Social Security Trust Funds are scheduled to reach $1 trillion by the year 2000 and $12 trillion by the year 2030. By the year 2025, it is projected that Social Security will pay out more than $3.5 trillion in benefits each year, about $10 billion a day.

If a box were filled with $1 trillion on the day Johann Gutenberg invented the printing press in 1436, and if you spent $1 million every day since then, the box would still be almost full! And it would take another 2100 years to spend the rest of the $1 trillion.

- The benefits paid to retirees are substantial, currently averaging about $8,500 for a single retiree. Couples do even better. If both husband and wife worked, they both receive benefits, which typically amount to about $17,000. If one spouse did not work outside the home, the spousal benefit equals approximately half the basic benefit, for a total of about $13,000 annually.
- For many people in our society, Social Security is the basic source of retirement income.

Oddly enough for such a large and important program, there is substantial confusion about what Social Security actually is. This confusion dates to the earliest days of the program.

## IT'S NOT A PENSION, IT'S A RELIGION
**•••**

When it began, in 1935, Social Security was a startling innovation, running strongly against even middle-of-the road opinion in the United States, which still held to the "rugged individualism" of the frontier. President Franklin D. Roosevelt recognized that the basic program ran against the grain of the electorate, and that is why he set it up the way he did.

The founders "sold" Social Security to the people, and to Congress, as a system of insurance—hence the terminology of Old-Age and Survivors Insurance and the Federal Insurance Contributions Act. As Martha Derthick wrote in her 1979 book *Policymaking for Social Security:*

> "Insurance" was the central symbol of all these messages, and it was stressed precisely because it was expected to secure public acceptance. Because insurance implied a return for work and investment, it preserved the self-respect of the beneficiaries; because it implied a return in proportion to investment, it satisfied a widely held conception of fairness;

and because it implied the existence of a contract, it appeared sound and certain. . . .

Taxes became "premiums" or "contributions." Workers had "old age insurance accounts" in Baltimore. They were "paying for their own protection, building up insurance for their old age." To challenge the insurance analogy or resist using the terms was to show oneself an enemy of the program.

The original plan did call for something like a funded pension system, with taxes paid into "trust funds" that would be invested, earn interest, and pay benefits. This plan satisfied Roosevelt's desire for a strong link between benefits received and taxes paid. Roosevelt believed that "workers who paid payroll taxes were more likely to support programs which linked benefits to their work efforts." And while motivating the taxpayer, he thought that it would also "place the government under an obligation to pay the benefits."

However, even before the first benefits were paid in 1940, the system was changed to a "pay-as-you-go" basis, in which current benefits are paid out of current tax receipts. Instead of a pension system, in which people in their old age reaped the fruits of their own labor and savings, Social Security became a wealth transfer from the young to the old. *And this is what it has been ever since.*

One of the reasons for the switch was a concern that the building up of large reserves would dampen an already weak economy. In addition, the switch allowed the system to start paying reasonable benefits from the beginning, rather than starting with very small payouts and increasing them only as the reserves grew.

Another change took place before 1940 that further distanced the system from any individual effort. Upon the recommendation of a blue-ribbon advisory panel, the system was expanded to pay benefits not only to retired workers but also to their wives, widows, and children. The original Old-Age Insurance became Old-Age and Survivors Insurance.

Through all this, the basic thrust of the terminology did not change. The language of "insurance" and "contributions" provided valuable political cover. The charade of individual Social Security accounts gave every taxpayer a sense of ownership in the program. Here is how it was explained in the original brochure sent to workers by the Social Security Board:

> Beginning November 24, 1936, the United States Government will set up a Social Security account for you, if you are eligible. . . . The United States government will send checks every month to retired workers, both men and women, after they have passed their sixty-fifth birthday and have met a few simple requirements of the law. . . . The checks will come to you as a right.

At one point, an aide suggested to President Roosevelt that Social Security's new auditors were just wasting time keeping track of each individual's "contributions" and retirement "accounts." As related by historian Richard E. Neustadt, Roosevelt replied: "That account is not useless. That account is not there to determine how much should be paid out and to control what should be paid out. That account is there so that those sons of bitches up on the Hill can't ever abandon this system after I'm gone."

It worked then, and it's still working today. Through the years, conservatives have flailed against the inappropriate terminology of Social Security. During a 1961 hearing, U.S. Senator Wallace F. Bennett (R-UT) noted, "My idea of a contribution is something I myself take out of my pocket and hand to somebody. It is not . . . what somebody else takes out of my pocket, and I think this is a tax." Such grumbling failed to dent the public perception of the system.

Scholars who exposed what they regarded as the myths of Social Security learned to expect a swift, vigorous response from program executives, especially if the critics were liberals and could therefore be regarded as "natural friends" of the system. Then they would be charged with heresy and made to feel that they were endangering the system. In 1976, economist Jodie Allen wrote a

# How Social Security
# Was Sold to the Workers
•••

Here are some excerpts from *Security in Your Old Age,*
the first publication of the Social Security Board.

## What This Means to You

This means that if you work is some factory, shop,
mine, mill, store, office, or almost any other kind of
business or industry, you will be earning benefits that
will come to you later on. From the time you are sixty-
five years old, or more, and stop working, you will get
a Government check every month of your life, if you
have worked some time (one day or more) in each of any
five years after 1936, and have earned during that time
a total of $2,000 or more.

The checks will come to you as a right. You will
get them regardless of the amount of property or income
you may have. They are what the law calls "Old-Age
Benefits" under the Social Security Act. If you prefer to
keep on working after you are sixty-five, the monthly
checks from the Government will begin coming to you
whenever you decide to retire.

## The Amount of Your Checks

How much you will get when you are sixty-five years
old will depend entirely on how much you earn in wages
from your industrial or business employment between
January 1, 1937 and your sixty-fifth birthday. A man
or woman who gets good wages and has a steady job

most of his or her life can get as much as $85 a month for life after age sixty-five. The least you can get in monthly benefits, if you come under the law at all, is $10 a month.

### Taxes

The same law that provides these old-age benefits for you and other workers, sets up certain new taxes to be paid to the United States Government. . . . The law also creates an "Old-Age Account" in the United States Treasury, and Congress is authorized to put into this reserve account each year enough money to provide for monthly payments you and other workers are to receive when you are sixty-five. . . .

During the next three years . . . you will pay 1 cent for every dollar you earn, and at the same time your employer will pay 1 cent for every dollar you earn, up to $3,000 a year. . . . Beginning in 1940, you will pay and your employer will pay 1½ cents for each dollar you earn, up to $3,000 a year. This will be the tax for three years, and then, beginning in 1943, you and your employer will each pay 2 cents for every dollar you earn for the next 3 years. . . . Beginning in 1949, twelve years from now, you and your employer will each pay 3 cents on each dollar you earn, up to $3,000 a year. This is the most you will ever pay.

critical article for *The Washington Post* entitled "Social Security: The Largest Welfare Program." She later described the response:

> I was deluged by calls and letters from the guardians of the Social Security system . . . saying, "Gee, Jodie, we always liked you but how could you say this?" I acted very politely, and I said, "Well, what's the matter with this; isn't it true?" And they said, "Oh, yes, it's true, but once you start saying this kind of thing, you don't know where it's going to end up." Then I came to perceive that Social Security was not a program; it was a religion. It's very hard to reform a religion.

## YOU CAN'T ARGUE WITH SUCCESS
**•••**

And, from the very beginning, it was an extremely successful religion. The first beneficiary of the program was Ida Mae Fuller of Ludlow, Vermont. On January 31, 1940, she received a Social Security check for $22.54. The retired law clerk continued to receive benefits for the next thirty-five years, until her death shortly before her hundredth birthday. In all, she had "contributed" $22 to the system; her benefits totaled $20,000.

During Ida Mae Fuller's thirty-five years of retirement, the system went from success to success. Benefits grew, taxes stayed low, the percentage of workers in the program expanded, and disability and health insurance were added to the old-age and survivors programs. This growth was supported by favorable demographic and economic trends.

### Demographics
Social Security was designed during the Great Depression, when America had lots of young people and relatively few old people— and the old people tended not to live very long. Consequently the burden of the wealth transfer was not very heavy. In fact, even before benefit payments started, the system was able to postpone the tax increase orginally scheduled for 1940; in the end, the rate

did not increase until 1950. The initial payment of benefits, originally scheduled for 1942, was moved up to 1940.

## The Economy

World War II ushered in a period of extraordinary prosperity for the United States. Until the 1970s, wage rates increased more rapidly than prices. As workers prospered, they paid more taxes into Social Security, helping to create annual surpluses and giving program administrators the political credibility they needed to expand the system.

And expand it did. Benefits increased dramatically. The average monthly Social Security check was $22.63 in 1940; $43.86 in 1950; $118.10 in 1960; and $341.71 in 1980. For 1991 the average check is $602—more than twenty-six times the 1940 payment.

Beginning in 1950, the system's coverage also expanded rapidly. Major legislation in that year extended coverage to many categories of workers that had not been covered earlier. Numerous additional extensions of coverage were enacted in succeeding years, and today more than 95 percent of American workers pay into and are covered by Social Security.

The percentage of older people receiving benefits skyrocketed, from 16 percent in 1950, to 82 percent in 1970, to 90 percent in 1980. (Older people, in this case, are people aged sixty-five or over. This definition actually understates the reach of the system, because, as we will see later, most people take early retirement—before sixty-five.)

Major new programs were also added to the Social Security system. In 1956 disability insurance benefits were added, and in 1965 the Medicare program was enacted. Today, 40 percent of the benefits paid from Social Security taxes are for purposes other than the retirement of a worker: disability and support of widow/widowers and children.

Meanwhile, taxes stayed low. The initial tax was 1 percent on the first $3,000 of wages, for a maximum payroll deduction of $30. (The employer paid an additional 1 percent, making a maximum total of $60 per year.) Both the tax rate and the tax base remained at their initial levels until 1950. In that year the rate went from 1 percent to 1.5 percent, and in 1951, the wage base —the amount of salary subject to the tax—increased from $3,000 to $3,600.

The tax rate and base continued to increase during the 1950s and 1960s, but remained very low. As late as 1971, the base was only $9,000, and the rate was 5.2 percent, for a maximum payroll deduction of $468.

With taxes at such low levels, any discussion of Social Security almost inevitably focused on the benefits, where there were votes to be had. Taxes were a nonviable issue, and could safely be ignored.

To a surprising extent, this is still true. When I became Social Security Commissioner in 1986, Secretary of Health and Human Services Otis R. Bowen, M.D., had these words of advice for me: "Remember, Dorcas, the checks must go out on time."

## COMING UNGLUED
•••

Beginning in the 1970s, however, changes in the underlying demographic and economic trends brought Social Security into a new era—an era where both taxes and benefits were at least intermittently on the political agenda. The easy growth of the early years was gone.

In 1950 there were sixteen workers for every Social Security recipient. By 1970 the figure had dropped to a little more than three workers for every beneficiary. And after decades of rapid economic growth and relatively low inflation, suddenly in the 1970s growth slowed and prices took off.

The situation was made worse by the indexation of Social Security benefits. In 1972 Congress, tired of enacting benefit increases every few years, passed legislation providing for annual cost of living increases, or COLAs. The first COLA was paid in 1975. It probably couldn't have come at a worse time.

The Social Security Administration had continued to make its projections on the assumption that wages would continue to increase more rapidly than prices. As events proved this assumption to be incorrect, the projections were recalculated, and the new forecasts showed that the system was in trouble.

In 1977 Congress faced the inevitable and virtually doubled the taxes. The increase was phased in, with the maximum tax going from $1,071 in 1978 to $1,975 in 1981.

As the final debate on the 1977 bill began, Al Ullman, Chairman of the Ways and Means Committee, addressed the House of Representatives. "There are not going to be any more easy votes on Social Security," he said. He was right.

## THE EIGHTIES—REFORM
## AND STALEMATE
**...**

In retrospect, the 1977 changes to the Social Security system illustrate the difficulties of making long-range actuarial projections. The package, which had been touted as putting Social Security back onto a sound footing for the next fifty years, proved very quickly to be insufficient.

Predicting the future is always a risky business. The health of Social Security rests on underlying factors that can and do change, and if the underlying factors change enough, then the program has to change as well. In the early years of the program, the underlying factors—demographics and the economy—were favorable, and changes were positive, such as the postponement of the first tax increase from 1940 to 1950, or moving the first payment of benefits to 1940 from the original 1942. By the 1980s, however, the underlying factors that had worked for Social Security in its early years were working against it, and the surprises, when they came, tended to be unpleasant rather than pleasant.

The early 1980s found the country mired in the worst economic downturn since the Great Depression of the 1930s; employment was way down, and Social Security tax revenues were missing their targets.

For the five years ending in 1982, actuarial projections had been for a 28 percent cumulative increase in inflation, an increase in real wages of 3 percent, and unemployment of 5.9 percent. The actual figures were very different. Cumulative inflation was more than 50 percent. Real wages in fact declined by 7 percent, and unemployment ran at 7 percent.

In this situation President Ronald Reagan appointed a bipartisan National Commission on Social Security Reform, chaired by economist Alan Greenspan (who now heads the Federal Reserve Board). In its recommendations, the commission actually nibbled at benefits, proposing a six-month COLA delay in addition to a variety of tax increases. It also proposed (for the first time) to tax the benefits of some retirees with high incomes.

The commission's proposals were adopted by Congress in 1983 as a "permanent" solution to the problems of Social Security. The actual results have been, financially, massive surpluses due to the subsequent economic expansion, and politically, a massive stalemate.

The Social Security trust fund surplus is projected to be running nearly $50 billion a year in 1995 and more than $100 billion a year in 2010. Unfortunately, the system then goes into deficit, and before the year 2020 it is projected to be running more than $100 billion a year in deficit. Figure 1.1 illustrates that the inclusion of Medicare (HI) makes the situation even worse.

Projections indicate that the combined systems would not go into deficit until after 2010, but there will be an obvious impulse to use Social Security's current surpluses to bail out the Medicare program.

I think this is a very bad idea. First of all, the combined bill that will come due after 2010 is almost unimaginably huge. It seems unfair for the current generation of elderly to once again mortgage its children's future to pay for its own benefits. Second, the basic problem in Medicare is runaway costs. Providing health care to the elderly is a serious issue that needs to be addressed

## FIGURE 1.1

### Projected Social Security Budget Deficits and Surpluses (Tax Income Less Outgo) in Nominal Dollars: 1991–2060

| Year | OASDI* | HI† | Total |
|------|--------|-----|-------|
| 1991 | 34.7 | 7.5 | 42.2 |
| 1995 | 48.3 | −2.9 | 45.4 |
| 2000 | 73.6 | −27.7 | 45.9 |
| 2005 | 101.0 | −63.6 | 37.4 |
| 2010 | 109.0 | −128.4 | −19.4 |
| 2020 | −127.4 | −429.50 | −556.8 |
| 2030 | −667.80 | −1,689.4 | −1,732.1 |
| 2040 | −1,201.2 | −2,037.0 | −3,238.3 |
| 2050 | −2,065.1 | −3,481.5 | −5,546.7 |
| 2060 | −4,090.8 | −6,096.8 | −10,187.6 |

Source: 1991 Annual Report of the Board of Trustees of the Federal Old-Age and Survivors Insurance Trust Fund and the Federal Disability Insurance Trust Fund. Alternative II.
* Old-Age, Survivors, and Disability Insurance Trust Funds.
† Hospital Insurance Trust Fund (Medicare, Part A).

today, and not swept under the carpet. Finally, Social Security needs to focus on its basic job of providing income security for the elderly and disabled. This is particularly true because Social Security, despite the "permanent" reform of 1983, faces serious issues that need to be addressed *today,* and not in the years after 2010.

However, since 1983 it has been extremely difficult to get people to pay attention to the issues that confront Social Security. The surpluses provide the illusion that all is well—at least until 2010. In addition, another factor has loomed large on the political stage in the 1980s, and that is the political power of the elderly.

Since the early 1980s, the Democrats have profited greatly by depicting the Republicans as a threat to Social Security. In the 1982 congressional elections, Representative Claude Pepper

(D-FL) crisscrossed the country, appearing before groups of senior citizens to support Democratic candidates, alleging that the Republicans wanted to put Social Security on the chopping block. Pepper's campaigning had a major impact on the election, in which the Republicans barely held onto their majority in the Senate and lost a net of twenty-six seats in the House.

Social Security was again an issue in the 1986 congressional elections. Of all those who voted, 38 percent were fifty-five years old or older. Republicans lost their control of the Senate, dropping a total of eight seats.

But they learned their lesson. In the 1988 presidential election, Representative Jack Kemp (R-NY) said that any candidate who proposed to tamper with Social Security was a "candidate for a frontal lobotomy."

The power (some call it arrogance) of the gray lobby is perhaps best illustrated by the story of the Medicare Catastrophic Coverage Act of 1988. The act was the first major revision of the Medicare system since it began in 1965, and it addressed what was perceived as the most significant gap in Medicare coverage, the failure to provide extended benefits for old people who required hospital care for long periods of time.

The most important provision of the new law was full coverage for hospital stays, no matter how long they lasted. Under the old law, payments were limited to the first sixty days of a hospital stay. In the words of President Reagan, the Catastrophic Coverage Act was designed to "help remove a terrible threat from the lives of elderly and disabled Americans, the threat of an illness requiring acute care, one so devastating that it could wipe out the savings of an entire lifetime."

The new law came with a twist, however. The elderly would benefit from the program, but they would also pay for it.

For the Medicare system, this was not a novel concept. Since the beginning, Medicare has been divided into Part A and Part B. Part A covers hospital charges and is paid for out of Social Security taxes. Part B covers doctors' fees and other nonhospital costs, and has always been funded in part by a deduction from the retired person's Social Security check. (The rest of the money comes from the general revenues of the federal government.)

In 1988 the monthly deduction was $27.10. The new act proposed to add four dollars to that figure. In addition, well-to-do retirees were assessed a surcharge on their federal income tax.

Although the legislation was supported by major senior citizen organizations, the act was so vigorously opposed by individual elderly that in 1989 Congress reversed itself and repealed the Medicare Catastrophic Coverage Act. Most observers insist that this demonstrates that the elderly are "greedy geezers" who always want a free ride. To the contrary, when the elderly understood the provisions of the law, they were unwilling to finance a program which they neither needed nor wanted. And they made sure their view was heard in Washington!

Congress once again learned its lesson, and in the congressional election year of 1990, no proposals concerning retirees got out of committee. As Representative Leon E. Panetta (D-CA), chairman of the House Budget Committee, put it, "If any changes on Social Security are proposed, multiply the protests against the catastrophic program by two!"

## ENDURING MYTHS
•••

The basic position of the elderly, of course, is that they have already paid, and now it is the turn of the younger generation. Social Security's continued reliance on such misleading terms as "insurance" and "contributions" and "trust funds" fosters the impression among young and old alike that Social Security is a funded pension system, in which retirees are merely being paid back, with interest, the "contributions" they made during their working years.

Social Security has never been such a funded pension system. Rather, it has always been a system whereby current workers support current retirees. In the early days, when taxes were low, it was easy to increase benefits. Now, however, taxes are high, and there is a need for the political system to balance the benefits enjoyed by the old against the tax burden borne by the young.

Another myth encourages even the young not to worry about Social Security, and that is the myth surrounding the surplus that Social Security currently enjoys. There is a feeling that, even if Social Security had not been a funded pension in the past, the reserves built up over the next twenty years will in fact provide income to cover the deficits projected to occur after 2010.

Unfortunately, this simply isn't true. The surplus is real enough, but it is not being invested to create a reserve that could help us in the years after 2010. Instead, it is being siphoned off to pay current government expenses.

Social Security tax revenues are invested in special-issue Treasury bonds. These bonds pay interest, and if the federal budget were running a surplus instead of a deficit, they would in fact constitute a reserve that could be drawn against in the future.

However, because the federal budget is running a deficit of several hundred billion dollars a year, the Treasury will not have any cash on hand to pay off the bonds that Social Security is holding. In order to redeem the bonds, the Treasury will have to ask Congress to raise taxes.

After 2010, we will have a choice. If we redeem the bonds, people still working at that time will have to pay higher income taxes. If we don't redeem the bonds, they'll have to pay higher Social Security taxes—or recipients will have to take lower benefits.

The basic point is that the current surplus is being spent now. It's not being put away in a reserve.

## THE OUTLOOK
...

In a sense, Social Security is a victim of its own success. It has been so successful for so long that people, even today, are unwilling to believe in anything but a happy future. Success has also led to an exaggeration of its capabilities and an overreliance on the program. Sooner or later, though, we're going to have to face facts. Sooner would be better.

When I became Commissioner of Social Security in 1986, I started out by stressing the financial integrity of the system and promised that the dollars would be there for everyone when they retired. But as I learned more about the future and watched Congress struggle to balance the budget, my enthusiasm became tempered. I began to limit the time span of my assurances to "as long as you live" when the audience consisted primarily of those already receiving or about to receive benefits. When speaking to younger groups, I limited my promise to the year 2010 "or so." And I tried to warn them that, in some circumstances, the crunch could come even earlier.

# T W O

........

# MYTHS:
# WHAT *IS* SOCIAL
# SECURITY?

Social Security is a program that touches almost everyone in this country, and yet remarkably few people have a clear idea of what it actually is and how it actually works. Some of the misconceptions are, in fact, startling; more to the point, if we want to fix Social Security, we first need to clear away the underbrush to see what's really there.

Here are some of the most common misconceptions:

**Myth #1. Social Security is a pension fund. Workers (and their employers) pay in taxes—or "contributions"—and when the worker retires the government returns this money in monthly Social Security checks.**

**FACT:** As we saw in the last chapter, the very first recipient of Social Security, Ida Mae Fuller of Ludlow, Vermont, contributed a grand total of $22 to the system—and received benefits totaling $20,000. (She lived to be ninety-nine years old.)

Today, in almost every case, every retiree gets back *all* of his own taxes in three or four years. From then on, the retiree is receiving what amounts to a government dole!

For example, a sixty-five-year-old worker who has paid taxes on the maximum amount of covered earnings throughout his or her career will have paid $34,000 in Social Security taxes through 1990. If that worker retired in January 1991, he was eligible for a Social Security benefit of $1,022 per month, and could expect to recover his total tax contribution in less than three years. And with a nonworking spouse, the benefit would increase to more than $1,500, and the recovery period would be even less.

This new pensioner is also likely to live for twelve to fourteen years, giving him total lifelong payments of $160,000 for the individual and nearly $250,000 with a nonworking spouse—and that's before cost of living adjustments.

### Myth #2. Social Security payroll taxes are kept in trust funds; each individual has a special account.

**FACT:** Contrary to popular opinion, there are no special individual accounts—no shoe boxes with workers' names holding money in a Baltimore vault.

All Social Security benefits are paid from taxes on current workers. Social Security is like a pipeline: taxes from today's workers flow in, are invested in special U.S. government bonds, and then flow out to current beneficiaries. You can call this a pay-as-you-go system or a pass-through system.

The fact remains, the taxes you pay today are not invested for your future retirement; they are primarily used to pay benefits to current retirees.

### Myth #3. The system has made ample provision for the retirement of the baby boom generation, which will begin around 2010 and will create a surge in the demand for benefits.

**FACT:** The system is currently running a surplus, which is invested in special-issue U.S. Treasury bonds that pay interest but are not marketable. The system's accumulated "reserve" is now about $200 billion; it is projected to be $1 trillion in the year 2000 and as much as $12 trillion by 2030.

These are enormous sums. Unfortunately, what we are looking at is a shell game. When the U.S. Treasury trades its bonds for the cash produced by the Social Security tax, it is in effect giving the Social Security system an IOU. This IOU is backed by the full faith and credit of the federal government, but not by anything else. There is no sinking account or special reserve at the Treasury where funds are accumulating to repay the IOUs. What this means is that, in 2010, when the Social Security system needs to tap its reserves, the Treasury will be unable to pay. It will have to turn to Congress and ask Congress to raise the money.

Where has all the money gone—these billions and trillions of reserve Social Security dollars? They are used to fund normal government operations. Until 1990, they were even used to make the federal deficit look smaller; however, legislation in 1990 forced a change in bookkeeping practices to separate Social Security, which is why the official deficit numbers took a big jump that year.

If the Smith family constantly borrows from Susan's College Trust Fund account to pay off credit card charges, when it comes time to send Susan to university, there will be no money in the account. IOUs do not pay tuition. Neither will they pay Social Security benefits.

**Myth #4. If we lower payroll taxes now, Social Security will go broke in a few years.**
**FACT:** It doesn't really matter. The surpluses being accumulated now are being spent now—on regular government operations. If there's a rollback of payroll taxes, as some in Congress have proposed, the effect will be to reduce the cash available for current government operations, not future Social Security benefits.

A rollback in Social Security taxes would provide one more

incentive for Congress to do something about the federal deficit, but it would not change the basic situation in Social Security.

Current taxpayers support current retirees. In 1990, there were three taxpayers supporting each retiree. By 2030, if current projections hold, there will be only two workers for each beneficiary. And by 2050, there will be only one worker for each beneficiary.

These hard demographic facts are bad news for the baby boomers. As they start to retire, around 2010, there is going to be a devastating crunch. Inevitably, either benefits will decline (in real dollars), or taxes will increase. In all likelihood, both things will happen, as politicians seek to spread the pain.

## Myth #5. Social Security stimulates the national economy.

**FACT:** This is half true. Social Security benefits do, Social Security taxes don't.

The benefits stimulate consumption to the tune of **$32 million each hour or more than $20 billion each month.** However, the taxes are a drain on the workers and employers who pay them. Retirees spend the money. Workers and employers would be far more likely to save and invest at least a part of it, which would be better for the economy.

The surpluses that the system currently enjoys are not really a savings because the money is used to fund current government operations. Once again, this is consumption and not investment.

## Myth #6. Social Security taxes and benefits favor the high wage earner and discriminate against the lower-income worker.

**FACT:** The tax is regressive, but the benefits are progressive. This means that the tax falls most heavily on low-income workers. It also means that these low-income workers are the ones who benefit most from the system when they retire.

The current tax rate is a flat 7.65 percent for all wages and salaries up to $53,400 a year. Earnings above that amount are not taxed (except for Medicare, which is a separate subject). So someone who earns $100,000 a year pays less, on a percentage basis, than someone who earns $10,000 a year.

Even someone who makes $50,000 a year is better off than someone who makes $10,000 a year. They're both taxed at the same rate, but the $3,825 the high earner pays is presumably less of a burden on him than the $765 that the low earner has to squeeze out of a budget where virtually every dollar goes for necessities.

That's why the federal income tax is a progressive tax, with people who make more money paying a higher percentage of their income.

The Social Security tax is more like a sales tax. The extra $10 on a warm winter coat probably doesn't pinch somebody making $50,000. For somebody making $10,000, it may make a difference.

On the other hand, lower-income workers benefit more from Social Security when they retire. Benefit payments are computed using a formula based on wage-replacement ratios. Persons with low incomes will receive benefits equal to 90 percent of their working wages. Those with the highest taxable income—$53,400 —will receive benefits equal to only 19 percent of their salary. And if they earned $100,000 a year, the effective wage replacement ratio is even lower.

This system of regressive taxes and progressive benefits reflects the origins of the Social Security system: that a social insurance program should contain elements of both individual equity and social adequacy.


**Myth #7. The sole purpose of Social Security is to provide benefits for senior citizens.**
**FACT:** In addition to retirees, the system provides benefits to survivors and the disabled. Of the nearly 40 million current beneficia-

ries, 3 million are disabled individuals under the age of sixty-five. Approximately 2.6 million children under the age of eighteen also benefit directly from Social Security payments, because they are surviving members of a family where the primary wage earner was qualified for benefits. There are 6 million adult survivors.

### Myth #8. Most people work all their lives to be able to spend a few years in retirement.

**FACT:** On the average, an individual spends only half of his or her life in the labor force. The first twenty years of life are for childhood and schooling; the last twenty are for retirement. In between are forty years of work.

This is a situation unprecedented in human history. In the past, most of an individual's life was spent at work. Schooling ended early, and when people retired they were generally very near the end of their lives.

Modern science has granted most of us a long and healthy life. There's also no doubt that a modern technological society needs us to spend a lot of time in school if we are to become productive members of the work force. But can society afford to have people spend only half their lives working, and all their lives consuming?

*If the answer is no, then the retirement age should increase.*

### Myth #9. Current beneficiaries paid the taxes that helped to create and maintain the program. It's only fair that the young continue to maintain the program as their elders built it.

**FACT:** Fairness is a two-way street. In essence, Social Security is a wealth transfer from the young to the old. In the past, the burden on the young was relatively light because there were so many of them, and there were so few old people.

Now, however, the old part of our population is growing very rapidly, and the working-age population is, relatively speaking, shrinking. The vast sums being transferred from the working population to retirees are already creating severe inequities that favor senior citizens at the expense of younger workers.

In 1991, more than half of America's workers and more than 70 percent of our families were paying more in Social Security taxes than in income taxes.

At present, the young are bearing this burden with a certain amount of good cheer. After all, as they pay their taxes they can often look within their own families and see the benefits. But when a high-earning couple that pays Social Security taxes of about $11,000 realizes that each set of their parents receives up to $18,000 for more than fifteen years (an awesome total of nearly $1,000,000 with cost-of-living adjustments), one wonders how long this cheerfulness will last.

# THREE

·············

# A WAR BETWEEN THE GENERATIONS?

The baby boomers rebelled against their parents in the 1960s. Will they do it again in the 1990s? If they do, the battle will almost certainly be over Social Security—first taxes, then benefits.

Until recently such a prospect was unlikely. After all, people may wince when they look at their pay stubs and see the amount withheld under FICA. But as long as they think they are investing in their own future, it seems like a good deal.

However, once you understand that the taxes you're paying are *not* being set aside for your retirement—that in fact the money is spent almost as soon as it is paid in to the government—then the perspective begins to shift. Soon the working taxpayer finds himself in a new world, a world that requires him to pay heavy taxes now, and also to face the relative certainty of low benefits later.

Meanwhile, the current generation of retirees is enjoying a prosperity unknown to previous generations and unlikely ever to return again. This prosperity does not derive from hard work and savings in years gone by. Rather, today's retired people are living on a government dole, and that dole is paid for by the sweat of people now working—the baby boomers in particular.

The way it's currently set up, Social Security is a lot like a chain letter—with the baby boomers holding the broken end of the chain.

## WHO ARE THE BABY BOOMERS?
•••

The baby boom began in 1946. World War II ended in 1945, and GI Joe came home to make love, not war. The result was an astounding jump in the production of babies, made even more precipitous because relatively few children had been born in the previous years of war and the Great Depression.

More than 3.4 million babies were born in 1946, a 20 percent increase over 1945—and that was only the beginning. The number of babies kept growing until it reached a peak of 4.3 million in 1957. After that, it tapered off, but births remained above 4 million per year through 1964, the last year of the baby boom.

Births were in the range of 3.1 million per year in the early seventies; right now they are up a bit from that level to over 3.5 million a year.

The total number of births has increased in recent years simply because there are so many baby boom women in their peak child-bearing years, not because the birthrate has gone back up. The typical baby boom woman continues to have fewer children than her mother (and she's also having them later in life).

Demographers use a number they call the fertility rate. This is the number of babies that a woman can be expected to have during the course of her life. (It is projected from the actual birthrate of a given year.) At the peak of the baby boom in 1957, the fertility rate reached 3.68. That's nearly four kids for every mommy during the Eisenhower years.

The fertility rate was still 3.17 in 1964, at the end of the baby boom. Then, in what is known as the baby bust or the birth dearth, the fertility rate dropped sharply, hitting 1.74 in 1976.

Today it is in the range of 1.8 to 2.0, about half of what it was in 1957.

## New Patterns

From the beginning, the economic lives of baby boomers have been very different from the experience of their parents. The boomers had grown up, typically, in a suburban household where Mom was a full-time wife and mother. Dad planned to work for the same company throughout his career, and frequently that's just what he did. It seems fair to say that the children, who had not lived through the excitement of the New Deal or World War II, found the prospect of replicating their parents' settled life-styles a trifle boring.

However, the new economic world of the baby boomers didn't come about solely because they felt like making a few changes, and made them. The two-career family didn't happen only because women wanted to have careers. The typical two-career family often *needs* that income. The second salary allows baby boomers to attain something approaching the prosperity of their parents.

Two incomes also provide the boomer family with greater security—in the event of a layoff, there's still one salary coming into the house. (Increasingly, the laid-off person may be a woman. Lee Hecht Harrison, a Manhattan-based outplacement firm, reported in 1989 that one in three laid-off executives was a woman, up from one in ten only five years previously.)

Again, boomer women are having fewer children than their mothers, and they're having them later in life. These changes are often attributed to the freedom provided by modern contraception and to women's preoccupation with their careers. However, the low fertility rate can also be a sign of an economic pinch as it was in the Great Depression. It's just possible that people can't *afford* more babies.

What will the boomers be like when they get to retirement? One of the positive aspects of the two-career family is that more baby boomer women will be collecting Social Security benefits in their own right, rather than the spousal benefit that derives from their husband's earnings. (In the last decade alone, the number of married women working has doubled.)

However, this bit of good news hasn't been able to sink an overriding sense of gloom about the future of Social Security. In fact, the public at large has grown rather pessimistic about the future of Social Security. In a 1988 public-opinion survey conducted by the U.S. Chamber of Commerce, 65 percent of those polled expected to receive benefits smaller than promised. (Of those over sixty-five, 35 percent expected to see their *own* benefits decline.) In addition, 61 percent of those polled believed that, unless Social Security is changed, today's students will not be able to collect Social Security benefits when they retire.

In other words, a lot of people think that Social Security is going to collapse. This is not an isolated finding. A 1985 survey, conducted by Yankelovich, Skelly and White, found that 66 percent of nonretired adults believed they would never receive Social Security retirement checks.

The reality is unlikely to be this bad. However, it will be bad enough. "The coming Social Security disaster will make the savings and loan fiasco look like child's play," says Walter Williams, a professor of economics at George Mason University. "Here are several realistic scenarios we face: When today's twenty-year-olds retire, they will receive pensions 50 percent less than those of today's Social Security recipients; many others will be excluded from receiving Social Security checks despite having made enormous contributions; if tomorrow's recipients are to receive pensions equal to today's, the 2020 work force will have to pay a 40 percent Social Security tax."

The checks won't go to zero, but they may get a lot smaller than projected. Currently the average Social Security check replaces 40 percent of the wages that the retired worker made before he retired. (The figure goes to 60 percent if the worker's wife claims the spousal benefit available to those who did not work outside the home.) As we saw in the last chapter, the size of this "wage-replacement ratio" varies considerably with the size of the

---

**FIGURE 3.1**

---

## Estimated Annual Benefit Amount for Single Retiree at Normal Retirement Age* with Average and Maximum Covered Earnings (Alternative II) 1995–2065

| Retirement Year | Current Dollars | | Constant 1991 Dollars | |
|---|---|---|---|---|
| | Average | Maximum | Average | Maximum |
| 1995 | 10,734 | 14,966 | 9,175 | 12,793 |
| 2000 | 13,669 | 19,802 | 9,604 | 13,913 |
| 2005 | 18,333 | 27,529 | 10,587 | 15,898 |
| 2010 | 22,483 | 34,792 | 10,672 | 16,514 |
| 2015 | 28,833 | 45,532 | 11,248 | 17,763 |
| 2020 | 39,786 | 63,034 | 12,757 | 20,212 |
| 2025 | 48,506 | 76,909 | 12,784 | 20,270 |
| 2030 | 60,594 | 96,073 | 13,126 | 20,811 |
| 2035 | 77,700 | 123,192 | 13,834 | 21,934 |
| 2040 | 99,644 | 157,866 | 14,582 | 23,102 |
| 2045 | 127,779 | 202,453 | 15,370 | 24,351 |
| 2050 | 163,862 | 259,614 | 16,200 | 25,666 |
| 2055 | 210,128 | 332,907 | 17,075 | 27,051 |
| 2060 | 269,473 | 426,919 | 17,998 | 28,513 |
| 2065 | 345,567 | 547,467 | 18,970 | 30,053 |

---

Beneficiaries are assumed to have been full-time workers earning the average wage in covered employment, or the maximum covered wage throughout their working lives. Married couples with a spousal benefit would receive 150% of the amounts shown in the table.

* Normal retirement age gradually moves from 65 to 67 after the turn of the century. *1991 Annual Report of the Board of Trustees of the Federal Old-Age and Survivors Insurance Trust Fund.*

worker's salary. A very-low-income worker will receive as much as 90 percent of his former wages when he retires; a high-income worker will receive as little as 19 percent.

In the next century, the wage-replacement ratio is going to

go down. The only question is how much. This stark fact has begun to elicit some reactions in Congress, and the 1988 Chamber of Commerce survey indicates that a constituency for reform is beginning to build within the electorate. Respondents to the survey favored raising the retirement age and cutting the payroll tax, and 46 percent wanted to make Social Security voluntary. It seems fair to say that this public constituency for change is still latent, but it is nonetheless real.

## A Look at the Older Generation
**• • •**

While the baby boomers tack and luff through what should be the peak earning years, let's take a look at the older generation they're supporting. Here the sailing is smoother than it has ever been.

The traditional view of the elderly was that they were poor, ill, dependent, and not likely to be around very long. In the early 1980s, as Jerry Gerber and his coauthors note in the 1989 book *Lifetrends,* this image underwent a rapid transformation. Old people, who had been portrayed as eating dog food because they couldn't afford anything else, were suddenly seen as a prosperous and powerful group intent on increasing their own welfare at the expense of other groups in the society. Society's "pathetic victims" had suddenly become "powerful parasites."

Stereotypes aside, the truth is that there's good news about old age. In general, older people nowadays are healthy, affluent, independent, long-lived, and—yes—politically influential.

Today, there are 31 million Americans age 65 or older, roughly 12 percent of the population. In 1900, only 4 percent of the population was 65 or older. The fastest-growing segment of the elderly population is the Old-Olds—those over 85. In 1990, there were 3.2 million people in this age bracket. In the last fifty years, a person's chances of living to 85 have doubled; by the year 2000, chances will triple.

Life expectancies have increased throughout this century. A

male born in 1910—and thus eligible for full Social Security benefits in 1975—had a life expectancy at birth of 48.6 years. One born in 1920, and turning 65 in 1985, could count on living 54.6 years. And one born in 1930—and thus not eligible for full benefits until 1995—had a life expectancy at birth of 59.7.

Note that, actuarially, not one of these men would have lived long enough to receive benefits! This was one of the secrets to Social Security's success in the early years. Now, however, the situation has changed dramatically. Let's look at some combined numbers for both sexes. In 1900, the life expectancy at birth for all people was 47.3 years. In 1985 it was 74.7 years.

Of those who live to 65, the increase in longevity has been equally startling. A man who turned 65 in 1935 could expect to live another 11.9 years; a woman who turned 65 in the same year could expect to live another 13.2 years. By 1990, life expectancy at age 65 had jumped to 16.0 years for men and 19.2 years for women.

## Health

Not only are people living longer, they're healthy longer. Between the ages of sixty-five and seventy-four, only about one in nine reports chronic health problems that prevent normal activity.

This is not to say that we have discovered the fountain of youth. Older people do have their infirmities—30 percent of those over sixty-five are hearing impaired, and 10 percent have severe visual problems, and, especially from the mid-seventies on, people do find that they have less energy, and they need to slow down.

With much-improved health comes increased independence. Contrary to popular belief, only about 5 percent of the elderly are in nursing homes at any one time. (The figure is much higher for the Old-Olds, of course. Of people over eighty-five, 22 percent are in nursing homes at any given time.)

## Wealth

By and large, older people have the money they need to enjoy life. Social Security is basic to the prosperity of the older generation, of course. However, many of those currently retired have also profited greatly from the extraordinary run-up in housing prices over the years. By selling their big old house and buying a smaller one, or a condominium, many of the elderly have created a sizable nest egg.

Baby boomers are unlikely to benefit from a similar increase in housing prices. The underlying cause of the run-up was the great demand for housing created by the baby boomers as they set up independent households. Because the generation that follows them is so much smaller, this situation will not repeat itself.

Here is how Amanda Bennett put it in an article for *The Wall Street Journal:* "Our parents benefited from the golden period of prosperity: college under the GI Bill, subsidized post-war housing with low down payments and cheap interest rates. Now we are the ones buying those houses, at triple the cost of our parents. It's tough to do this even with two paychecks, and we realize there won't be much profit when we sell."

Current retirees also benefited from the stock market, where the Dow-Jones industrial average soared from 631 to almost 3000 during the 1970s and 1980s. Properly invested, even modest savings grew substantially. These investments, coupled with the profits from the sale of one's home, have allowed many people to retire in recent years with nest eggs of $250,000 or more.

Older people constitute only 20 percent of America's households, but they own 40 percent of the nation's wealth. Average assets per retiree, including home equity, are $68,000. Fully 70 percent of retirees own a house or a condominium, and on 80 percent of those houses there is no mortgage. Families headed by a person sixty-five or older have a median income of $20,000 per year, 40 percent of which comes from Social Security.

### And a Few Are Poor

Some old people are poor, just as some old people are sick. In 1985, 12.6 percent of all persons sixty-five and older were officially classed as poor. Generally speaking, couples did better than single people, and poverty increased with age; the group that was worst off was older women living alone.

The official statistics almost certainly overstate the true burden of poverty among the old. If full allowance is made for the special benefits available to the elderly, only 3 percent of those between sixty-five and eighty-five are actually poor. (Even with these revised figures, however, poverty continues to be a serious matter among those over eighty-five, where the rate is 15 percent.)

And the government has always had difficulty dealing with the question of what constitutes poverty in rural areas, where food and other necessities often come from the land rather than the store.

For example, in Florida, a retired worker and his spouse live happily in an agricultural area with a total income from Social Security of $9,000. Indeed, they insist they've never had it so good. Their $9,000 income is more money than they ever made while they were working, and they feel financially secure. They have their own home and with it a garden, citrus trees, and a lake for fishing. They are eligible for nutritious, pay-if-you-can meals at the local senior citizens' center, and they receive free or low-cost medical care. Their taxes are minimal. They pay no income taxes because they are below the threshold for federal levies. They pay sales taxes only on nonfood items. And they pay little in the way of direct taxes to the state and local governments because Florida exempts the first $25,000 of *assessed* valuation from property taxes.

There are some critics who refuse to face the reality that our retirement programs have *already* transformed old age. These critics continue to focus on bureaucratic definitions of poverty, and they propose to establish a minimum stipend for all older Americans whose cash income is below a certain level. However, the Supplementary Security Income (SSI) program already exists to provide a safety net for the elderly poor. For those who qualify, SSI does extend a helping hand with a monthly check.

Said a 1989 report from the congressional budget office, "Broad measures of economic status indicate that the elderly as a group are doing relatively well. Since 1970, their median income has grown faster than that of the nonelderly. Their poverty rate has fallen to an all-time low and is now less than that of the rest of the population."

## Political Muscle

Politicians seem to concentrate unduly on the relatively small number of old people who are sick or needy, and ignore the nearly 90 percent who are doing just fine, thank you. This can lead to a distortion of priorities.

"The real problems of poverty involve single mothers of small children," notes Michael Novak, who directs social and political studies at the American Enterprise Institute. Between 1970 and 1985, poverty among those sixty-five and older dropped from 24.6 percent to 12.6 percent. Meanwhile, during those same years, the percentage of children living in poverty increased from 14.9 percent to 20.1 percent.

Of course, children don't vote; older people do. In fact, the elderly are widely recognized as the most potent voting bloc on the American political landscape today. Their power reaches its peak in presidential election years, because more than half of the elderly in this country reside in eight states that are crucial to anyone who hopes to get to the White House: California, Florida, Illinois, Michigan, New York, Ohio, Pennsylvania, and Texas.

In 1960, only 6 percent of federal expenditure went to the elderly. Today, the elderly benefit from 32 percent of all federal expenditures. This is not an accident.

# A Brief History
# of Early Retirement
...

Another sign of the political power of the elderly is contained in a paradox: at the same time that they've been growing healthier, they've also been retiring earlier.

At the turn of the century, two thirds of all men sixty-five and over were still working. As late as 1948, well after Social Security had begun paying retirement benefits, nearly half of all men sixty-five and older were still in the labor force.

Today, however, five out of six men in the sixty-five-and-older age bracket are retired. And that's not all. In the 1950s and 60s, Congress amended the Social Security Act to allow for early retirement—as early as sixty-two—and today 70 percent of all workers start collecting benefits *before* the age of sixty-five.

In 1940, when Social Security started making payments, people were spending about 7 percent of their lives in retirement; today the figure is around 23 percent. And, as we've seen, these are generally years of healthy, active retirement.

The Social Security Administration expects the trend for early retirement to continue until the year 2000. In that year, because of legislation enacted in 1983, things are going to start to change. In 2000, the normal retirement age, now sixty-five, will start a gradual increase, reaching sixty-six by 2009 and sixty-seven by 2027. Everyone born after 1937 will be affected. (Early retirement at sixty-two will continue to be available. However, the reduction in benefits will increase as the normal retirement age increases.)

The changes are a major shift in the orientation of Social Security, which was set up fifty years ago to deal with the problems of a world that was very different from the one that we now live in. At the time, it made sense to encourage retirement because there were many younger workers ready to take the place of those who left the work force. In fact, some scholars argue that the primary purpose of Social Security was to make jobs for the young, not to improve the life of the old.

Whatever the reason, Social Security has (until now) always sought to encourage retirement, and it has been very successful not only in getting the older generation to retire, but in getting it to do so at an earlier age.

Such a bias may have been appropriate in 1940, when the system was set up, but it is clearly inappropriate now, for two main reasons. First, people simply don't get old as early as they used to. Second, instead of facing a major surplus of labor, the country is already seeing the beginnings of a significant labor shortage that will only grow in the coming years. So the 1983 changes in retirement age were the right thing to do from a public policy point of view, as well as from the fiscal responsibility point of view.

The remaining question is—why so little, and so gradually? Under the current setup, the changes in retirement age will have a significant effect only on the baby boomers. The current generation of retirees gets off scot-free.

## How It Might Happen
...

The year 1989 may prove to have been the high-water mark for the elder lobby. That was the year in which America's retirees took a hard look at the Medicare Catastrophic Coverage Act of 1988 and decided they didn't want what was offered at the price they were asked to pay.

This may cause other people to start asking why *they* should pay. The trigger may be the 1991 increase in Medicare taxes—although the rate stays the same at 1.45 percent, the base goes to $125,000. (The cap for the other components of the FICA payroll reduction is much lower—$53,400.) The impact will be greatest upon the young and middle-aged executives who are the leaders of public opinion, the most likely candidates for Congress, and a major source of financing for political campaigns.

Will America's working taxpayers finally decide that they've had enough? Will the baby boomers dust off their activism of the sixties and march on Washington?

Already the baby boomers are aware that Social Security is in trouble, and that *their* benefits are in jeopardy. Will they soon see that money saved on Social Security now is money that could be diverted to savings and investment now?

To date, baby boomers have shown little interest in Social Security. This is partially because most people continue to view it as a funded pension system, rather than the pass-through system that it actually is. When they understand that the money for today's retirees comes not from yesterday's taxes, but from today's taxes, will they be as cheerful about the annual benefit increases?

When they understand that the huge surpluses the system is currently running are being diverted to pay for current government operations, and will not be there for them in the next century, how will they react?

Increasingly among baby boomers, there is the somewhat wistful perception that their parents have had it better than they ever will. When does wistfulness turn to demand for change?

## IF THE BABY BOOMERS DON'T
## THE BABY BUSTERS WILL
### •••

The baby boomers will be doing a major public service if they do put the issue of Social Security into play, because if they don't, the intergenerational stresses in our society are only going to continue to build.

Today, the baby boomers are making money and paying taxes. When they retire, in the early years of the next century, they will look to the generation of the baby bust to support them as they are now supporting the current generation of retirees.

There are lots of baby boomers. There are relatively few baby busters. The ratio of workers to retired people, which has already declined dramatically in recent years, will plunge further. In 1989 there were 3.4 workers for every retiree. By the year 2010 that figure will drop to 3.0, and by 2030 there will be only two workers for every retiree.

The number of people aged sixty-five and older will increase from 31 million today to 60 million in 2025. They will make up 19 percent of the population then, compared to 12 percent now.

The Old-Olds—those over eighty-five—will increase from 3.2 million in 1990 to 7 million in 2025; 75 percent of these Old-Olds will be single, divorced, or widowed and therefore very likely to need extensive government assistance.

The total number of Social Security beneficiaries—the elderly, survivors, and the disabled—is expected to increase from around forty million in 1990 to fifty million in 2010; to sixty-five million in 2020; to seventy-five million in 2030; and to eighty million in 2050.

Expenditures will double every ten years, until we talk about trillions the way we used to talk about billions. Current benefit payments are now $275 billion; they will be $500 billion at the turn of the century, and $20 *trillion* by 2050.

Michael J. Boskin is a former Stanford University professor who is now chairman of the president's Council of Economic Advisers. In his 1986 book *Too Many Promises—the Uncertain Future of Social Security,* he painted the potential for economic war between the baby boomers and the baby busters in bleak terms.

> When the baby boom generation retires . . . hard-pressed workers will certainly resist tax rate increases of 5, 10, or 15 percentage points. The larger elderly population, meanwhile, will push for these tax increases to finance not only existing benefits, but also new ones. A confrontation between workers and retirees will arise (involving trillions of dollars) that will create the greatest polarization along economic lines in our society since the Civil War.

## Racial Overtones

There is also the potential for this conflict between baby boomers and baby busters to take on racial overtones. The reason is that retirees will still be overwhelmingly white, and workers will increasingly belong to various minorities.

At present about 90 percent of older people are white. The proportion of older minorities will increase, from the current 10 percent to about 21 percent in the year 2030, but because of immigration and differential birth rates, the minority population will grow much faster at younger age levels.

By the year 2000, nearly a third of the total population of the United States will be minority, including thirty-six million blacks, eight million Asians, and thirty-five million Hispanics. By 2030, when 21 percent of the older population will be nonwhite, 41 percent of the children will be minorities.

Hispanics are growing five times faster than the rest of America. Already Mexico has replaced Germany as the number one country of ancestry for America's foreign-born residents.

At present, Latins and Asians make up about 80 percent of the approximately six hundred thousand people who immigrate to the United States every year. Many of these people are relatively unskilled, and they work hard at low-paying jobs. Social Security taxes will be a heavy burden for them.

The dream of the American immigrant remains what it always was—a better life for the children. Central to that better life is education—an increasingly expensive commodity in the United States. As we move into the next century, will the minorities of this country—immigrants and otherwise—come to see the Social Security system as a mechanism by which the government robs their children of a better future, in order to support a group of elderly white people in a retirement that is both too luxurious and too long?

# FOUR

··········

# SOME PROPOSALS FACING CONGRESS

Even now there are signs that the logjam in Congress is beginning to break up. Currently circulating among legislators are a number of thoughtful proposals that share the goal of improving the Social Security system. All these plans recognize that the present system simply will not provide the benefits that have already been promised to the baby boomers for their retirement. Many share a recognition that the burden of taxes on current workers is inequitable. However, from this common recognition that there is a problem, the proposed solutions branch off in many different directions. What follows is a review of the most important initiatives currently being discussed.

Although health care financing is beyond the scope of this book, the impending deficits in Medicare pose a threat to the Social Security system, because there will soon be intense pressure to raid the Social Security retirement fund to bail out Medicare. A similar but smaller problem will arise with the Social Security disability fund, which is expected to be in trouble by the end of the decade. In a brief note at the end of this chapter, I suggest that borrowing from the old-age and survivors fund to cover these deficits is a very bad idea.

# THE MOYNIHAN TAX CUT
•••

U.S. Senator Daniel Patrick Moynihan (D-NY) is widely regarded as one of Washington's most thoughtful legislators. He is chairman of the Social Security subcommittee of the Senate Finance Committee, and in the early 1980s he was a member of the bipartisan National Commission on Social Security Reform. This was the commission whose recommendations formed the basis for Congress's 1983 overhaul of the Social Security system.

Senator Moynihan's basic proposal is to roll back Social Security payroll taxes to the levels of the early 1980s. This would put Social Security entirely back onto its original pay-as-you-go basis, eliminating the huge surpluses that the system is currently running and will continue to run for the next twenty years or so.

Senator Moynihan and Senator Robert Kasten's (R-WI) proposal has the great merit of eliminating the sham that surrounds these surpluses. Many people think they add an element of a funded pension system to Social Security—that the money will be available to cover the deficits that the system will surely encounter in the years after 2010. As we have seen, however, this money is actually being used to pay for current government operations, and in the years after 2010, we will confront a simple choice—raise Social Security or other taxes, or decrease benefits.

In the Moynihan plan, the FICA payroll deduction would be cut by 1 percent. All of this cut would come from the old-age, survivors, and disability portions of the tax, reducing them from 6.2 percent to 5.2 percent. This cut would be equally applied to the employer payroll tax. The Medicare portion would stay the same at 1.45 percent, so the total tax would decline from 7.65 percent to 6.65 percent.

To cover any deficits Senator Moynihan would raise the taxable earnings base to $82,200 by 1986 and schedule new tax increases for 2012, 2015, and 2055.

The multibillion-dollar tax cut called for in this plan would be a significant relief for middle-income individuals. Those paying the maximum levy of $5,123 would see a reduction of around $600.

The senator believes strongly that it is unfair to use Social Security taxes to reduce the federal deficit. Even though a 1990 change in accounting procedure means that the government can no longer use Social Security funds to make the official deficit look smaller, the money continues to be spent for current government operations.

Although the senate rejected the Moynihan proposal for 1991, the senator vowed to bring it back. "Don't be surprised if it takes ten years," he said. "It will come."

# REACTIONS TO
# THE MOYNIHAN PROPOSAL
...

Economic forecaster Jeffrey Bell gave the Moynihan initiative a generally favorable review in the *Wall Street Journal:*

> The massive payroll tax increases of the past dozen years were enacted in 1977 and 1983 when the system was about to run out of money because of the stagflation of the 1970's. This harmed Social Security in two ways: benefits go up because of inflation but contributions stay low because of slow employment growth. The tax writers of 1977 and 1983 assumed continued stagflation [and] enacted a series of huge tax increases: from a maximum of $740 a year to $7,516 (half by the employer) to keep the system afloat. But they reckoned without the Reagan expansion which added nearly 20 million workers to the payroll tax system without significant infla-

tion. This led to massive overfunding which, says the Senator, should be partially returned to taxpayers and accompanied by a substantial tax cut. These actions should spur job creation and business expansion by reducing fixed costs, for most businesses, by 18%.

The Congressional Research Service has proposed an alternative that would allow Congress to eliminate the taxation of Social Security benefits and also the earnings limit on retirees under the age of seventy.

What the Congressional Research Service has suggested is to cut the payroll tax 0.1 percent less than Senator Moynihan has proposed. This would generate enough money to allow Congress to eliminate both the taxation of benefits and the earnings limit. The taxation of benefits provision has been unpopular since it was enacted in 1983; and the earnings test is widely seen as limiting elders' participation in the work force at a time when the nation faces a growing shortage of labor.

The Moynihan proposal has also aroused opposition in influential quarters. Alan Greenspan is presently chairman of the Federal Reserve Board. A decade ago he chaired the bipartisan National Commission on Social Security Reform, of which Senator Moynihan was also a member. Says Mr. Greenspan, "The Senator has properly diagnosed a crippling national problem but has prescribed the wrong medicine."

Former senator William Armstrong (R-CO), who also served on the commission, says "Pay-as-you-go sounds fiscally responsible; it's really attractive, but to the extent that Social Security is a form of forced savings, the Moynihan proposal goes in the wrong direction."

What Mr. Greenspan and Senator Armstrong and others are worried about is the federal budget deficit. The direct impact of the Moynihan proposal would be to reduce the federal government's receipts by $100 billion a year. Although this would no longer affect the official deficit figure (because of the 1990 changes in bookkeeping procedures), it would decrease the government's cash flow. If the money is not raised in taxes, then it will have to be raised through debt—selling bonds to the public.

One solution would be for Congress to balance the federal budget, but this doesn't seem likely to happen any time soon.

Part of the current debate centers on whether the Social Security surpluses should be seen as going simply to consumption —current government operations—or whether they should be seen as encouraging national savings and capital formation. Some authorities suggest that, because the income means the Treasury needs to sell fewer bonds to the public, money is freed for investment in private enterprises.

This argument ignores the basic fact that Social Security is supposed to pay for Social Security, not the daily operations of the federal government. And, in terms of economics, it fails to recognize the stimulative effect of a tax cut—the average taxpayer could undoubtedly find productive uses for the money, if only the government would let him hold on to it in the first place.

Fiscal Associates of Washington, D.C., has analyzed the results of a reduction in the payroll tax of 2.2 percent (half for the employee and half for the employer). This is slightly larger than the cut proposed by Senator Moynihan. This research group found that, over the next twenty-one years, such a tax cut would "raise economic growth by 0.6 percent, creating 930,000 new jobs, $346 billion in increased GNP, and a $162 billion increase in the stock of U.S. capital."

The Heritage Foundation, a conservative think tank, supports the Moynihan proposal. Says Vice President Kate O'Beirne, "With the threat of a Medicare bailout and the inability of Congress to cut spending, the only way to go is the tax cut; dollars should remain in the private sector where they can be productive."

# THE GRAHAM-MATSUI REROUTE
**...**

At present the Social Security surplus is invested in special-issue Treasury bonds. As we have seen, when the federal budget is in deficit, this leads to a shell game. The Treasury siphons the money off to pay for current government operations, and in exchange it gives Social Security an IOU. When the IOU comes due, there will be no money in the Treasury to pay it off, so one way or another, at that point, Congress will have to raise revenue.

The situation would be different if the surplus were invested in projects that could pay the money back. Senator Bob Graham (D-FL) and Representative Robert T. Matsui (D-CA) have suggested that we invest the money in rebuilding America's infrastructure—roads, bridges, and other projects funded by state and local bond issues.

Under the Graham-Matsui proposal, investment decisions would be made by the trustees of the Social Security system on the recommendation of a "state and local government obligations investment committee." The diversified portfolio would include only high-grade government bonds. Because such bonds often carry at least a partial tax exemption, they are likely to pay less interest than U.S. Treasury bonds. Annual appropriations from federal general revenues would be used to cover the difference.

## Investing in Private Securities
There seems no reason why the Graham-Matsui proposal couldn't be extended to include investment in private securities.

On a smaller scale, this concept of government investing in private corporations has already been successfully implemented with the assets of the Pension Benefit Guaranty Corporation, which manages pensions for employees of bankrupt corporations.

Obviously, any assets invested in the private sector—whether in stocks, corporate bonds, or real estate—would have to be handled carefully, because, with the vast sums of money involved, significant parts of the nation could wind up coming under government ownership—a kind of back-door socialism.

However, other nations have successful programs in which government-sponsored retirement programs invest in private enterprises. With strict guidelines the United States, with its marvelous skills in finance, could undoubtedly develop an effective blend of public and private investments.

## MR. PORTER WOULD PRIVATIZE
...

Representative John Porter (R-IL), a member of the House Appropriations Committee, thinks he has a better idea for the future of Social Security. He would refund 2 percent of the total taxes to the individual taxpayer who would be required to invest it for his retirement. This scheme goes by the name of "privatization."

Privatization creates a new kind of savings for retirement—the government requires the individual to save money for the future, but the individual retains control over how the money will be invested. Thus it is somewhere in the middle between Social Security (where the individual's tax dollars leave his control) and an Individual Retirement Account (where the individual is encouraged but not compelled to save for his retirement).

Privatization directly addresses the basic problem of Social Security. The current system simply will not have enough money to pay benefits at the present level when the large baby boom cohort retires. Baby boomers need to build their own nest eggs. Privatization forces them to do this, at least to an extent.

Each year, under the Porter plan, the government would deposit 2 percent of a worker's Social Security taxes into a personal pension plan, called an Individual Social Security Retirement Account (ISSRA).

Each worker would own his or her own account, investing and reinvesting the assets over a working lifetime. Investment safeguards would be established, and, as with Individual Retirement Accounts, ISSRA funds could not be withdrawn prior to retirement. Workers could negotiate an additional employer contribution to their ISSRAs as their company's retirement plan.

These funds would be immediately vested, protected from possible future employer or union pension fund fraud or bankruptcy, and would be completely portable as the employee moves from job to job.

Congressman Porter projects that every worker "would become an investor in our economy and have a direct stake in its success. In addition, a tremendous foundation of domestic savings and investment would be built under our economy that would help remove us from heavy dependence on foreign capital." He also argues that denying the federal government the Trust Fund reserves by placing them in ISSRAs "would discipline the system and ultimately help to bring down interest rates and stimulate economic growth."

Politically, Congressman Porter acknowledges that "anyone who wants to change Social Security has a tough road," but he is determined to continue to push his plan.

## Other Privatization Plans

Several other plans for Privatization of Social Security are circulating. They are quite similar to the Porter plan. In all, Social Security would continue to have first call on all of its receipts, so that there would be ample funds available to pay benefits, maintain contingency reserves, and defray administrative expenses. Only the excess could be used for private investments.

One plan calls for setting aside 20 percent of total Social Security taxes; another would require a minimum percentage of taxes plus a sliding scale for persons with higher income. A third would establish a flexible allocation schedule to be determined annually by the Secretary of Health and Human Services. There are also differences in the proposals for payment of retirement benefits.

Even the private sector has begun to take the leadership to develop alternatives. The Merrill Lynch Company, an international brokerage and financial services firm, has developed a proposal whereby a portion of the Social Security tax is deposited into personal accounts and available for retirement, long-term care insurance, or even education, allowing employees to regain control of their own future.

## The Gephardt Proposal

In a further wrinkle, Congressman Richard Gephardt (D-MO) has proposed to refund to all workers 10 percent of their annual Social Security taxes. The refund, however, would come from the general Treasury and not from the Social Security trust funds. To stimulate economic competitiveness, he would also restructure the FICA tax so that it applies to unearned income from dividends, interest, and capital gains, not just wages.

# HOW PRIVATIZATION MIGHT WORK
### •••

Here is an example of how privatization might work. In order to keep the calculations relatively simple, we will assume that the plan calls for the privatization of 20 percent of Social Security taxes (not counting the Medicare premium).

The year is 1992; the worker is Henry Hardapple, age forty. At that time, he is earning $40,000 a year. Every five years, Henry gets a raise of $10,000, so he is up to $90,000 in 2016. He retires in 2020, at age 70.

The example assumes that Henry is taxed on his full salary throughout his career. In addition to a rising base, the example assumes one rate increase, in 2001. The rate goes from 6.2 percent (exclusive of Medicare) to 7.55 percent. (In reality, rates will probably increase more than once.)

Under a privatization plan, Henry receives a refund of 20 percent of his Social Security taxes, which he invests at an annual rate of return of 10 percent. His total investment over the years is $28,230. With compounding—and no taxes—his investment grows to the tidy sum of $118,323: enough to assure him and his spouse some $12,000 a year for as long as they live

These are Henry's dollars, so he can be sure of them. How much income he can expect from Social Security is, as we have

## FIGURE 4.1

### Privatization of 20% of Social Security Taxes

| Years | Salary | S.S. Taxes | 20% Private | Annual Contributions Factor: 5 Years: 6.11 | Single Sum Factor |
|---|---|---|---|---|---|
| | | | | | 25 years: 10.83 |
| 1991–1995 | $40,000 | $ 2,480 | $ 496 | $3,031 | $32,826 |
| | | | | | 20 years: 6.73 |
| 1996–2000 | 50,000 | 3,100 | 620 | 3,788 | $25,493 |
| | | | | | 15 years: 4.18 |
| 2001–2005 | 60,000 | 4,530 | 906 | 5,536 | $23,141 |
| | | | | | 10 years: 2.59 |
| 2006–2010 | 70,000 | 5,285 | 1,057 | 6,458 | $16,726 |
| | | | | | 5 years: 1.61 |
| 2011–2015 | 80,000 | 6,040 | 1,208 | 7,381 | $11,834 |
| 2016–2020 | 90,000 | 6,795 | 1,359 | 8,303 | $8,303 |
| Total Contributions: | | $28,306 | Total Nest Egg for Retirement: | | $118,323 |

seen, an uncertain thing. My guess is that, although Social Security took 80 percent of his taxes, the 20 percent that Henry invested for himself will probably give him more income in retirement.

## PETE DuPont's Idea
•••

Pete DuPont is a former governor of Delaware, and in 1988 he was a candidate for the presidency. He has offered a somewhat different approach to privatization, which he calls the Financial Security Program.

Under the DuPont plan, everyone would continue to pay FICA taxes. However, a worker would have the *option* to participate in the Financial Security Program by contributing to a personal Financial Security Account. The contribution could equal but not exceed the amount that the worker paid in FICA taxes. For every dollar invested in such an account, the worker would receive an equal federal income tax credit.

The DuPont plan is estimated to cost at least $20 billion a year in lost income taxes. However, every dollar of tax credit would be matched by a dollar of new savings in FSAs.

## RAISING THE RETIREMENT AGE
•••

A. Haeworth Robertson, former chief actuary of the Social Security Administration, suggests that the normal retirement age be raised to seventy in the very near future.

Mr. Robertson's plan also calls for a uniform Social Security payment to everyone, regardless of previous employment and earnings history or financial need. Annual adjustments would be maintained; all benefits would be subject to income tax.

These adjustments on the spending side do not eliminate Social Security's crunch on the income side, and so Mr. Robertson proposes a new source of income for the Social Security trust funds.

He suggests that the federal government issue Freedom Bonds. These would provide Social Security with immediate income, and they would provide investors with retirement income. They would be zero-coupon bonds with an effective annual rate of appreciation of 10 percent, tax deferred.

Individuals would be allowed to purchase these bonds between the ages of forty-five and seventy. Every year they would be allowed to invest up to a maximum of 10 percent of their total earnings—$5,000 for an executive making $50,000 a year.

Freedom Bonds could be redeemed in the event of death or disability, or upon retirement at age seventy. The payout could be a lump sum in cash or a lifetime annuity.

## SLOWING THE GROWTH OF BENEFITS
•••

"The only alternative is to slow the growth of benefits," says Dr. Aldona Robbins, a Social Security expert and a former senior economist with the U.S. Treasury. She suggests changing the way the benefit formula adjusts for inflation, from the current wage indexation to price indexation (price indexation is the system already used to adjust the brackets of the federal income tax). Such a change was originally recommended by William Hsiao, a Harvard professor, during the debate leading to the 1977 amendments to the Social Security Act.

Real benefit levels under the price-indexing alternative would rise more slowly than under the present system of wage-indexation. Benefit levels would double rather than triple in real terms over the next seventy-five years.

Initially the savings would be small, because only new retirees would be affected, and the difference in their benefits would be negligible. Noticeable differences would begin to appear only when the baby boom generation begins retiring, around 2010.

Stephen J. Entin, a resident scholar at the Institute on the

Economics of Taxation and a former deputy assistant secretary of the U.S. Treasury, agrees with Dr. Robbins on the advisability of switching from wage to price indexing. He would also like to see the retirement age raised to seventy-two, with benefits for early retirement reduced proportionally.

## DR. BOSKIN'S TWO-TIER APPROACH
•••

Michael J. Boskin, chairman of the president's Council of Economic Advisers, has urged Congress to undertake a major overhaul of the Social Security system, rather than continuing to "lurch from crisis to crisis." In his 1986 book *Too Many Promises—the Uncertain Future of Social Security,* he suggests a two-tier approach, similar to the system recently launched in the United Kingdom. He would separate the insurance and welfare components of Social Security, tie benefits directly to taxes paid, and guarantee a minimum level of retirement income for all citizens.

## THE OUTLOOK
•••

Perhaps the most significant aspect of all these proposals is that they are actually being made and considered. Even a year ago, Social Security was untouchable. Now, however, politicians are beginning discussions of the Social Security system and its future. Although major changes may not occur immediately, we are in the early stages of a much-needed great debate; Social Security taxes, as well as benefits, could become issues which are discussed calmly in future elections.

# Growing Support for
# Social Security Reform
···

According to a recent poll by the Employee Benefits Research Institute, the idea of Social Security reform is gaining support:

- 59 percent deemed Social Security programs *very* important;
- 45 percent said participation in Social Security should be voluntary;
- 81 percent disapproved of lending Social Security tax revenue to the government to pay for defense, education, or other programs;
- 49 percent favored applying a portion of their Social Security taxes to Individual Retirement Accounts.

Additional education of the working population could have a tremendous impact.

## A NOTE ON FINANCING
## DISABILITY AND MEDICARE
···

In 1981, Social Security's old-age and survivors trust fund was so broke that Congress authorized it to borrow money from the disability trust fund and from the hospital insurance trust fund (Medicare Part A). In 1982 the OASI fund did borrow a total of $17.5 billion. After Congress enacted major changes in Social Security in 1983, the health of the OASI fund began to improve, and it repaid the loans in 1985 and 1986.

Now the disability and hospital funds are in poor shape. In their 1990 report, the trustees of the disability fund said that it might be "depleted in 1998 in the absence of corrective legislation." The HI fund, for Medicare Part A, is in even worse shape, with deficits predicted as early as 1992 under the most pessimistic assumptions. Serious trouble by 1995 seems almost certain.

Very shortly these looming deficits are going to put Congress under intense pressure, and Congress is very likely, in these circumstances, to turn for relief to the old-age and survivors fund, which is currently running a very large surplus.

There are two things wrong with this picture. First of all, as I have tried to point out in this book, Social Security has serious problems of its own *right now,* and it needs to concentrate on its basic job of providing retirement income for the elderly. Second, both Medicare and the disability program are in need of reform. A loan will simply allow Congress to avoid facing the music for a few years; meanwhile, the money will be frittered away.

Of the two funds, disability faces the most tractable problems and the most manageable deficit. Medicare, on the other hand, is a much larger program. Despite recent reforms, costs continue to escalate very rapidly, and the deficits that are projected for the coming years are simply awesome. Congress should find effective solutions for these problems now, and not paper them over, hoping that the sun will shine on a coming day.

# FIVE

·········

# MY RECOMMENDATIONS
*Dorcas R. Hardy*

I have two main recommendations: First, when it comes to Social Security, we need to live in a world of facts, not myths. Second, the government, business leaders, and individuals must work together to develop a comprehensive national retirement policy.

The earlier chapters of this book have attempted to strip away some of the most misleading myths that continue to surround Social Security and to set forward the hard facts that we will need to confront if we are to develop sensible solutions to the real problems of the Social Security system. However, if we concentrate only on Social Security, we will not solve the problem of retirement income.

Unfortunately, most people don't see Social Security as the base of a much larger retirement system that includes pensions and private investments. When I was commissioner of Social Security, I found that politicians in particular tended to concentrate on Social Security to the virtual exclusion of the other elements of the retirement system. Congress especially pays little attention to private savings, and too often it actually winds up discouraging such savings by statutory restrictions.

The history of Individual Retirement Accounts provides a good example. Congress established IRAs in 1974, and in 1981 it greatly expanded the number of people who could have them. The program was so successful that the loss in tax revenue after 1981 was six times greater than had originally been estimated. Instead of seeing this as a sign of success, Congress decided to see it as a problem and, in the Tax Reform Act of 1986, severely limited the tax incentives associated with IRAs. Not surprisingly, people are now putting less money into IRAs—although it's still a very substantial program. And Congress continues to scold the public for a low savings rate.

In the future, we're going to have to do a better job of looking at all the sources of retirement income, and making sure that they work together as a coherent, effective system. Above all, we need to recognize that, in the future, Social Security will inevitably play a much smaller role in retirement income than it does today.

## SOME POLITICAL REALITIES
...

As we develop a comprehensive national retirement policy, we need to recognize a few hard political realities.

*1. There will be no significant reductions in the benefits paid to current retirees.*

Seniors frighten elected officials. It may be possible for politicians to nibble a bit around the edges, as was done in 1983, when cost of living increases were delayed six months. But the burden of any major reductions in benefits will be borne by people who have not yet retired.

We may even see some increases in benefits as new income streams are directed toward the elderly. In Pennsylvania, to pick only one example, the proceeds of the state lottery were dedicated to programs for the aging, with emphasis on new benefits such as free taxi service and drug prescriptions. (It's interesting to note that, when income from the Pennsylvania lottery exceeded expectations, additional uses were found for the funds. First the state directed the money to existing programs for the elderly—helping to pay for the state's portion of Medicaid. Later, some of the surplus was mingled with general revenues.)

*2. Seniors will resist paying higher taxes, even when the taxes are dedicated specifically to programs for the aging.*

This is the lesson of 1989, when intense pressure from the elderly forced Congress to repeal the Medicare Catastrophic Coverage Act of 1988. The episode cast neither the elderly nor Congress in a particularly favorable light, and Congress is likely to go to considerable lengths to avoid any similar fiasco in the future.

Once again, though, it may be possible to nibble around the edges. The 1983 reform of Social Security introduced the taxation of Social Security benefits. This was initially limited to beneficiaries with high incomes, but because the income limits are not indexed for inflation, this tax will affect more and more retired people as the years go by.

## GOALS FOR A
## RETIREMENT POLICY
...

The underlying goals of a national retirement policy should be made explicit. Here are a set that I think are reasonable. The policy should:

- Seek to ensure financial independence in retirement for all Americans.
- Reaffirm the concept of Social Security as the base for retirement income. Social Security will continue to provide benefits for almost all retired workers. For many, however, it will no longer be the main source of retirement income.
- Promote the expansion of the revenue pool available for retirement income. Congress is right: Americans should save more.

- Plan for a shifting mix of revenue sources. Two thirds of current beneficiaries rely on Social Security for 50 percent or more of their income. Other sources of revenue are simply going to have to play a larger role.

Most important, the policy should seek to promote individual responsibility. If people want a pleasant retirement, they are simply going to have to take a bigger hand in planning for it. They will need to become sophisticated about how they can save for retirement, they will need to learn how to manage a portfolio of future income sources, and they will have to bite the bullet and *save*. The policy must encourage people to step in aggressively and take responsibilities that they have largely surrendered to the government.

With these goals in mind, let us turn to specific actions.


## Recommendation #1. Balance the federal budget.

If Congress balanced the budget of the federal government, then the surpluses that Social Security currently enjoys would work as intended, providing a reserve to help pay benefits to baby boomers when they retire, in the years after 2010. As we have seen, with the federal budget in deficit, the Treasury simply siphons off Social Security's surplus for current government operations, issuing IOUs that are backed by the full faith and credit of the government, but nothing else.

If the federal government were running a surplus, it would be possible to set aside and invest reserves to pay off the IOUs when they come due. In such a situation, Social Security would be comfortably solvent for at least the next fifty years, in all but the most pessimistic scenarios.

Unfortunately, I have been in Washington for more than a decade, and despite initial optimism, I no longer hold out any great hope for a balanced budget soon.

**Recommendation #2. Use the current Social Security surplus for the benefit of future retirees.**

This is what most people *think* is happening now, and it's the right thing to do. The funds should not be diverted to current government operations, as they are now, nor should they be used to cover the impending deficit in Medicare.

Of the available alternatives, my preference is some form of **privatization**. Congressman Porter's proposal, discussed in the last chapter, is an excellent starting point. Each year, under the Porter plan, the government would deposit 2 percent of the payroll tax into a worker's personal pension plan, called an Individual Social Security Retirement Account (ISSRA). The Porter plan puts the Social Security surplus directly to work for future retirees. The other main alternatives are less direct.

Senator Moynihan's proposal would eliminate the surplus through a tax cut. This would effectively return the money to the taxpayers before they'd even parted with it. However, Senator Moynihan's proposal does nothing to encourage savings for retirement. The Graham-Matsui proposal would invest the Social Security surplus in projects that could pay the money back—a significant improvement over current arrangements. The proposal serves two purposes—the rebuilding of America's infrastructure and the protection of benefits for future retirees. It is possible, however, that in the future, these purposes could conflict.

The tax cut and investment proposals have some merits and it is not unlikely that a final program could contain elements of these two approaches, as well as privatization. Passage of any legislation is going to require the building of a grand coalition, and in the building of coalitions compromise is inevitable.

The most important thing is not to lose sight of the basic point, which is that Congress should use the current Social Security surplus for the benefit of future retirees.

## Recommendation #3. Modernize the Social Security retirement age.

If sixty-five was the proper retirement age in 1940, today, because of rising life expectancies, it should be seventy-three. A retirement age of sixty-five is now a luxury. We don't need it, and we can't afford it.

Most older people are healthy and vigorous well into their seventies, and this will be more true in the future. A logical step is to move the normal retirement age from sixty-five to sixty-seven, not in the scheduled thirty-five years (2027), but in three or four, and phase in an extension to age seventy by the 2020s. The early retirement option which 70 percent of beneficiaries now select, should be reduced by raising the minimum age from the current sixty-two. By the 2020s, early retirement should be eliminated completely.

## Recommendation #4. Eliminate the Social Security earnings penalty.

With the nation facing a labor shortage, nothing should be done to discourage older Americans from working.

During this decade we should change the incentives in Social Security which encourage older Americans to leave the workforce. With the nation facing a labor shortage, nothing should be done to discourage older Americans from working. A first step is to eliminate immediately the Social Security Earnings Test which penalizes retirees between the ages of sixty-five and seventy who earn too much income.

Concern has been expressed about the cost of such an elimination. After all, such a move would provide full benefits to people who are currently receiving only partial benefits. However, research indicates that the government would actually come out ahead if it eliminated the Earnings Test.

The National Center for Policy Analysis and Drs. Gary and Aldona Robbins developed an economic model for Congress that assessed the impact of eliminating the Earnings Test. They found that the federal government would be obligated to pay an additional $4.8 billion in Social Security benefits but would collect nearly $5 billion in additional work-related taxes. And these estimates do not include revenues previously uncollected from the vast "gray underground economy."

Both the revision of the retirement age and elimination of the earnings penalty would go a long way toward ensuring the solvency of the Social Security system.

## Recommendation #5. Encourage the growth of private pensions.

Of all the money that all the nation's retired people are currently receiving, only 15 percent comes from private pensions. And right now, the prospects for growth in this system seem meager. Since the mid-seventies, private pensions have risen only 3 percent, and with mergers and takeovers, scores of pension plans have been wiped out or replaced with annuities, which usually pay lower benefits.

At present only 45 percent of the private labor force is covered by pension programs, and if current trends continue, that percentage is likely to decline. Pensions are a way of life in large organizations. Not so in small companies, which is where the nation's jobs increasingly are located. There is also a perceptible shift from full-time to part-time employment, and part-time employees almost by definition do not receive the benefits available to full-timers.

Congress needs to take a hard look at pensions and how they fit the emerging world of work in America. The basic goal should be to encourage the growth of retirement income from pensions. The pot of money needs to grow, and the number of people covered needs to grow.

A cohesive agenda should be constructed around the following principles.

**1. Simplicity.** Congress should simplify the complex maze of pension laws and regulations that lead to prohibitive administrative and compliance costs for many employers. Both Congress and the IRS should stop making frequent, annoying, and costly changes to the system.

**2. Portability.** Today's American worker will change jobs eleven times during the course of his career. We need a pension system that allows the worker to carry vested assets with him when he changes jobs. This will be a big change for the pension system. One of the original goals of pensions was to encourage valued workers *not* to change jobs.

**3. Retirement at a Later Age.** The private system, like the public system, should stop encouraging early retirement. Normal retirement age should be congruent with that established for Social Security. Once again, this will be a big change for the pension system. At present almost half of all pension plans permit retirement at age fifty-five; the majority provide for only a small difference in benefits if the worker decides to retire at sixty-two instead of sixty-five. There are also penalties, or inequities, for those who work past normal retirement age: According to the Employee Benefit Research Institute, a private industry worker who delays retirement by five years can lose as much as 50 percent of lifetime benefits.

**4. Worker Education.** As I noted earlier, we need to encourage individuals to take responsibility and plan for their own retirement. They can't do this without information. Companies need to start the process well before workers attend those preretirement seminars. Financial reports also need to be simplified.

**5. A New Product Mix.** Any useful reform of the pension system will require a different mix of retirement plans. Congress should encourage Defined Contribution Plans (where the savings are the same percentage for everyone), especially those that include employee savings. It should phase out Defined Benefit Plans (where the annual contributions are set on the basis of the work payments), which are inequitable, costly, and increasingly financially unsustainable. Congress should also encourage the development of new products. Tax incentives could spur the financial services industry to create products that combine life and health insurance with asset accumulation for pensions, and to expand reverse annuity mortgages to make it easier for the elderly to tap the equity tied up in their homes. These are only two examples.

**6. Adequate Funding.** The current limits on annual contributions are too low in most pension programs. Limits should be higher, both for existing programs and for new programs.

### Recommendation #6. With or without the help of government, increase individual private savings.

The safest, surest, most logical solution for all future retirement income is to build your own assets by investments. Congress can help by restoring the full tax deductibility of Individual Retirement Accounts, by privatizing a part of Social Security revenues, and by reforming the private pension system so that it fits the needs of tomorrow and not yesterday.

In the end, though, the responsibility is yours. If you're planning on retiring after the year 2010, you need to recognize that a secure retirement is up to you.

There are things that you can do, *today,* to assure yourself of a financially secure retirement. They involve a program of serious and consistent savings, and then the wise investment of the money that you have saved. Even if you have only a moderate income, if you start now, you will be able to be financially secure when you retire. The next part of this book will show you how to do it. Read it now and start immediately.

# PART II

# Planning for Your Retirement

# TO BUILD YOUR NEST EGG, SAVE EARLY, INVEST IN QUALITY

To assure a steady flow of ample income after retirement, you must have substantial assets that pay dividends or interest and/or can be cashed in gradually. Success is easy when you start early, invest wisely, and are patient. Too many people scoff at the idea that slow and steady is the best way to build retirement funds. They are slow to save, take unwise risks in hopes of quick profits, buy popularity rather than profitability, and fail to recognize the importance of compounding, time, and quality.

The single most powerful force in long-term investing—as with pension plan assets—is *compounding:* prompt reinvestment of all income so that your money earns more money. As shown in Table 6.2, with an average annual rate of return of 10 percent, this strategy will: (1) with a single sum, double in value every seven years; (2) with the same annual contribution, compound by 57.27 in twenty years and by 164.49 in thirty years. This means that savings of $250 per month ($3,000 a year) will swell to almost half a million—$493,470—over a working lifetime. Such projections assume investments in a pension plan where taxes are deferred until withdrawal.

Note *the value of time:* in thirty years, annual contributions of $1,000, invested at 10 percent, will swell to $164,490, but a late starter who saves for only ten years, will have only $15,940. Note also *the impact of a higher rate of return:* at 8 percent, a single $10,000 investment, over twenty-five years, will compound to $68,500, but at 12 percent, will be worth $170,000.

With Social Security facing so many present and potential problems, it's clear that the only sure way to build a financially secure retirement is through your own savings. This should be done primarily through pension plans because of their tax advantages. However, personal savings, either directly or through annuities and insurance, can also play a substantial role.

Start with a disciplined plan. Try to save 10 percent of your net income every month by making out the first check to yourself —for your retirement plan. Invest in liquid assets (such as money market funds) until you have accumulated sufficient money to buy securities or shares of mutual funds.

If you start saving for retirement in your twenties, there should be no financial problems. If you wait until your thirties, you may have to rethink your goals. If you wait until your forties, there's still time. If you don't get started until your fifties, success is still possible, but it won't be easy.

To older folks, all these "rules" make sense. To younger folks, maybe not. In most cases, the people who will be retiring in the future will be quite different from their parents. Those born after 1928 didn't experience the Great Depression, and they have never known a world without Social Security. Someone born in 1928 turns sixty-five in 1993. So, really, there aren't that many people around who remember what it was like before Social Security—and virtually all of them are retired.

To provide a frame of reference, take a look at Figure 6.1, which is a table of life expectancies. The table tells you how long you can expect to live. It's important to recognize, however, that the figures in the table are averages; half of your age group will die before their projected age: for a sixty-five-year-old male, 15.2 years, to just over age eighty; for a female, 18.8 years, until nearly eighty-four.

| | **Male** | | **Female** | |
|---|---|---|---|---|
| **Age** | **Years To Go** | **To Age** | **Years To Go** | **To Age** |
| 55 | 22.3 | 77.3 | 26.8 | 81.8 |
| 65 | 15.2 | 80.2 | 18.8 | 83.8 |
| 75 | 9.4 | 84.4 | 11.9 | 86.9 |
| 85 | 5.4 | 90.4 | 6.5 | 91.5 |

**FIGURE 6.1**

**Life Expectancies**

*Source:* American Council of Life Insurance.

In 1990, the projected life span of a sixty-five-year-old male was 15.2 years, to just over age eighty. A woman, also sixty-five, can expect to live 18.8 years until nearly eighty-four.

If you are turning sixty-five in the year 2000, stretch the numbers a bit. If it's 2010, add one more year for men, and 1.5 years for ladies. Use these guidelines in your retirement planning, and then also make provisions to protect yourself and your loved ones in case you live to be 100.

Next, set dollar goals for your retirement income, and factor in the erosion caused by inflation. See Figure 6.2. This is a complicated-looking table, but once you learn how to use it, it's really quite simple. For now, we're only interested in the left-hand columns, the ones used to calculate the effects of inflation.

Let's say that it's 1990, and you're planning to retire in the year 2000. You talk with your spouse, and do a little figuring, and decide that you'd be happy with a retirement income of

---

### FIGURE 6.2

## All-Purpose Table for Calculating Inflation and Compounding Investment

| Annual Rate Years | (for inflation) 3% | 4% | Single Sum 5% | 6% | (for compounding) 8% | 10% | 12% |
|---|---|---|---|---|---|---|---|
| 10 | 1.34 | 1.48 | 1.63 | 1.79 | 2.16 | 2.59 | 3.11 |
| 15 | 1.56 | 1.80 | 2.08 | 2.40 | 3.17 | 4.18 | 5.47 |
| 20 | 1.81 | 2.19 | 2.65 | 3.21 | 4.66 | 6.73 | 9.65 |
| 30 | 2.43 | 3.24 | 4.32 | 5.74 | 10.06 | 17.45 | 29.96 |
| 40 | 3.26 | 4.80 | 7.04 | 10.29 | 21.72 | 45.26 | 93.05 |
| **Annual Contributions** | | | | | | | |
| 10 | | | | 13.18 | 14.49 | 15.94 | 17.55 |
| 15 | | | | 23.28 | 27.15 | 31.77 | 37.28 |
| 20 | | | | 36.79 | 45.76 | 57.27 | 72.05 |
| 30 | | | | 79.06 | 113.28 | 164.49 | 241.33 |
| 40 | | | | 154.76 | 259.06 | 442.59 | 767.09 |

---

*Inflation.* To protect the impact of inflation, multiply the dollars spent by the percentage opposite the years in the future. Thus, for every $1,000 spent in Year 1, with inflation at 3%, to buy the same goods/services, you will need: in 10 years, $1,340 ($1,000 × 1.34); in 40 years, $3,260 ($1,000 × 3.26).

*With a single-sum investment,* earning 10% annually, each $1,000 will grow, in 10 years, to $2,590 ($1,000 × 2.59); in 40 years, to $45,260 ($1,000 × 45.26).

*With annual contributions:* $1,000, at a 12% rate of return, in 20 years, will compound to $72,050 ($1,000 × 72.05); in 40 years, to $757,090 ($1,000 × 757.09).

---

$20,000 a year. Then, you estimate that inflation will average 4 percent over the next ten years. The factor is 1.48.

Now you take your desired retirement income of $20,000 and multiply by 1.48, which gives you $29,600. That is the amount of money you will need in the year 2000 if you want to have the same buying power as today. The effects of inflation can be a bit scary, but the compounding on your savings will be even stronger.

Third, make projections on the basis that you, as an individ-ual, are going to have to provide most of those dollars, with some help from your employer. Today, people rely primarily on Social Security—and why not? On average, it replaces 40 percent of the working income, and with the benefit for a nonworking spouse, the figure goes to 60 percent. In the future, the prudent planner will be looking to other sources for at least 75 percent of his retirement income.

## YOUR RETIREMENT GOAL
•••

Everyone has, or will have, a personal definition of "ample assets" for retirement. Most experts agree that a viable goal, in tomorrow's world, should be $500,000. Those retiring before the year 2000 can get by with less.

Such a goal can be achieved with savings of $1,027 a year for forty years. That's less than one quarter of what the average worker now pays for Social Security taxes. Over four decades, this $86 per month, invested at a 10 percent annual rate of return in a tax-deferred pension plan, will compound to that half a million dollars with a bit to spare. Those assets will provide an annual income of some $50,000 as long as you and your ever-loving live. Those future dollars won't buy as much as today, but with a nest egg of that size, there shouldn't be any financial problems.

To make these calculations, use Figure 6.2, starting with the anticipated rate of return, say 10 percent; then back to the number of years of savings. For 40 years, the factor is 442.59. Multiply the savings of $1,027 by 442.59 to get $454,539.93.

You can also work backward from your goal to find your needed annual savings. Let's say you have only thirty years to save $500,000. With a 10 percent annual rate of return, the factor is 164.49. Divide $500,000 by 164.49 to get $3,039.70 a year—about $250 a month. The later you get started, the more you have to save every month to reach the same goal.

Success requires regular contributions. With intermittent savings, you lose the full benefits of compounding. You can use the single-sum part of Figure 6.2 to calculate the results of intermittent savings. Let's say you put away $5,000 now and don't draw on it for thirty years. Find the 10 percent column, and use the single-sum part of the table, on the top. The factor for thirty years is 17.45. You get $87,250—a tidy sum, but not enough to pay for retirement.

Besides, it's not that easy to come up with a lump sum of $5,000. The best approach is to set your savings goals at an affordable level, and then save every month for as many years as you can.

## THE COST OF LIVING
**...**

It is also important to calculate the impact—good and bad—that inflation will have on your income after retirement.

First, let's take a look at Social Security's COLAs, which have been averaging about 4 percent in recent years. Let's say that Albert turns sixty-five in 1991 and retires. His wife, Lois, has not worked. Their joint benefits are $14,019. With annual COLAs of 4 percent, their joint benefits, in ten years, will be $20,748 (factor of 1.48). After twenty years, these will be $30,702 (factor of 2.19). If they both live to age eighty-five, they will receive more than $500,000 from Social Security . . . under our current conditions.

But inflation will reduce the true value of those dollars. With fewer needs, wise planning, and doing more things themselves, Al and Lois hold their costs of living to a 3 percent increase a year: for every $1,000 spent today, they will need $1,340 in ten years (factor of 1.34); in twenty years, $1,810 (factor of 1.81).

In planning and future execution, be realistic and do not kid yourself, or your partner, that expenses can be reduced sufficiently to offset inflation. Almost everything will cost more unless you are willing to change your life-style.

# SEVEN

∎∎∎∎∎∎∎∎∎∎∎

# SOCIAL SECURITY: STILL THE BASE

**D**espite the dire prospects for the continued viability of Social Security, be optimistic and start your retirement income projections on the basis of present benefits for yourself and spouse, as joint beneficiaries and as individuals, now and after the first death. For accurate projections, call the toll-free number: 1-800-772-1213 to request a Personal Earnings and Benefit Estimate Statement. This service is free.

---

### FIGURE 7.1

---

### Key Data on Social Security: 1991

|  | Monthly | Annual |
|---|---|---|
| Maximum Wage Base |  | $53,400* |
| Tax Rate: 7.65% each, employer and employee |  |  |
|     6.2% OASDI †    1.45% HI ‡ |  | 4,085 |
| Maximum taxes |  | 8,170 |

FIGURE 7.1 (*continued*)

## Key Data on Social Security: 1991

|  | Monthly | Annual |
|---|---|---|
| Benefits: at normal retirement |  |  |
| Average retired worker | $   602 | $  7,224 |
| Maximum at age 65 | 1,022 | 12,264 |
| 50% nonworking spouse | 511 | 6,132 |
| Total benefits | 1,533 | 18,396 |
| Both with maximum benefits | 2,044 | 24,528 |
| Aged widow | 557 | 7,224 |
| Aged couple | 1,022 | 12,264 |
| Disabled worker: spouse and one or more children | 1,022 | 12,264 |
| Supplementary Social Insurance (SSI) |  |  |
| Individual | 407 | 4,884 |
| Couple | 610 | 7,320 |
| Early Retirement Benefits |  |  |
| at age 62, 80% of those at 65 | 818 | 9,111 |
| 50% nonworking spouse | 409 | 4,555 |
| Total $ | 1,227 | 13,666 |
| Medicare |  |  |
| Premiums | $29.90 | $358.80 |
| Annual deductibles: |  |  |
| Part A |  | 592.00 |
| Part B |  | 100.00 |

*Source:* Social Security Administration.
* Subject to annual increases of the Consumer Price Index—projected to $67,000 by 1995.
† OASDI: Old-Age, Survivors, and Disability Insurance.
‡ HI: Medicare's Hospital Insurance.
§ Between age 62 and 65, early retirement benefits rise on a sliding scale. In the future, base age will move up to 67 and, in the next century, to 70.

Those retirement checks from Uncle Sam can be substantial—as much as $24,528 a year for a couple, both of whom have been working and earning the maximums over the years. The average is lower—$7,224 for an individual, $10,836 for a couple with a nonworking spouse.

If you retire early, as most people do, your benefits will be cut from the level you would receive if you waited until the normal retirement age of sixty-five. At age sixty-two, benefits are reduced by 20 percent. For persons retiring between sixty-two and sixty-five, the benefits increase on a sliding scale until they hit 100 percent at sixty-five.

Still, the checks undoubtedly encourage quitting early. For a beneficiary with a nonworking spouse, the maximum is $13,666 a year for life, plus COLAs. No wonder so many folks choose this option!

However, you can collect this amount only if you really retire. Some part-time work is okay, but if you earn too much, the system penalizes you by cutting your benefits. In the age bracket 62–64, the Social Security earnings penalty begins with an earned income of $7,080: for every two dollars you earn above that level, you lose one dollar in benefits. That's the equivalent of a 50 percent income tax . . . on top of what you are already paying. In the 65–69 age bracket, the base of earned income is $9,720. Above that, you lose one dollar of benefits for every three dollars you earn.

After the age of seventy there is no earnings test. You can make as much money as you want and still collect full Social Security benefits. Between sixty-two and seventy, though, the earnings test is a real deterrent to people who want to work. The good news is that there are proposals in Congress to eliminate the earnings test for those over 65. If you agree, you might want to write a letter to your congressman.

Figure 7.2 shows how to calculate reductions in benefits under the earnings test.

---

**FIGURE 7.2**

---

## How Earnings Affect
## Social Security Benefits (1991)

At ages 62–64, when earnings are above $7,080 a year, $1 is withheld from benefits for every $2 earned above that limit. At ages 65–69, $1 is withheld for every $3 earned above $9,720.

---

| | |
|---|---|
| Post-Retirement Wages | $10,000 |
| At ages 62–64: | |
| Excess over $7,080 | 2,920 |
| Reduction in S.S. benefits | 1,460 |
| FICA tax @ 7.65% | 765 |
| Total deductions | 2,225 |
| Net before income tax | 7,775 |
| At ages 65–69: | |
| Excess over $9,720 | 280 |
| Reduction in S.S. benefits | 93 |
| FICA tax @ 7.65% | 765 |
| Total deductions | 858 |
| Net before income tax | 9,142 |

After age 70, no penalties.

---

Do your homework before you blithely assume you can work to supplement your benefits: at $10,000 a year, a 63-year-old can lose $2,225, plus $2,800 in income tax. Add expenses for travel, meals, and clothing, and the net would be under $5,000!

# THE FUTURE
# OF SOCIAL SECURITY
...

Keep in mind that we've been discussing *current* benefits. In the future, the dollars will change, possibly lower, certainly with less purchasing power. It is unlikely that Congress will cut benefits.

Probably, COLAs will be reduced and more benefits will be taxed . . . or both.

*If you are over age 60, don't worry. The real crunch is not expected until after the year 2010. The decline in real benefits will impact on those born after 1937!*

Under recent legislation, the normal retirement age will start a gradual increase in the year 2000: to age 66 by 2009, to 67 by 2027. Early retirement will be available . . . with reduced benefits . . . but Congress may make further revisions and phase out this option!

What this means: the most vulnerable age group is now, and will be, those under age forty. Their Social Security benefits will be less: possibly in net dollars, certainly in purchasing power. That's why it is imperative that younger workers start building their own retirement nest egg so that, after retirement, these assets will provide almost all after-work income. Or, plan to keep on working. *Future Social Security will be insecure.*

# EIGHT

# PENSIONS: RETIREMENT PLAN PRIMER

All pension plans are controlled by federal law and regulations and, in some cases, by state requirements. The goal is to set up programs that will permit current contributions to a fund where the assets will grow, tax deferred, until withdrawal. Depending on the type of plan, the contributions can be made by the employer, the employee, or both.

These retirement savings plans must have a custodian and a trustee who is financially responsible for the investments and making regular reports to all participants and the IRS. Because the rules change frequently, it is essential to work with a knowledgeable adviser.

## EMPLOYER PENSION PLANS
...

Employer pension plans date back more than a century, but their growth accelerated during World War II when, with wages frozen, pensions became a popular way to reward workers. By the 1960s, retirement benefits were a major issue in union negotiations, and today they are an integral part of compensation with almost all government entities and more than half of private corporations—primarily those with more than one hundred employees.

These plans range from very good to very bad. When the employer makes all or a large portion of the annual contribution, the benefits can be worthwhile. In many cases, pension and Social Security, taken together, replace as much as 70 percent of the worker's income during the last year of work. These payments will continue for the lives of both worker *and spouse,* unless the worker signs away this provision, but may be reduced.

When pension plans are bad, the results can be devastating: inadequate funding leads to false promises and worthless IOUs. Such disasters often occur with corporate takeovers when shrewd operators loot the reserves, swap savings for annuities (promises to pay), recalculate pension liabilities, and reduce contributions.

For the employee, whether clerk or vice president, there's little protection unless the firm goes bankrupt. Then, some workers may be paid up to $27,000 a year by the Pension Guaranty Corporation. The probability of such support was recently enhanced by a court ruling that made a troubled corporation primarily responsible for benefits, thus freeing more funds for payouts.

The prospects for employer pension plans vary widely, depending on the plan and who you're listening to.

On the positive side, a report by Hewitt Associates on 392 of the nation's largest industrial corporations with Defined Benefit Plans found that, in 1989, 94 percent had pension fund assets that exceeded all future benefits they are obligated to pay their employees after retirement.

On the negative side, another study of pension assets of large organizations showed that, without the enhancement of interest and dividends, the annual contributions were not sufficient to cover the pension checks for current retirees. Almost all increases in fund assets were found to be due to capital gains in the ebullient stock market of the 1980s.

Major firms in the automotive and heavy machinery industries and several large cities, such as New York and Los Angeles, face rising fund deficits. If there should be a severe recession, many pension plans based on employer contributions may be unable to fulfill their promises to provide retirement income.

Do not despair. Many employer-paid pension plans provide excellent benefits. Figure 8.1 outlines the formulae used by a major industrial corporation. For one year's employment, for the $50,000-a-year executive, the annual benefit is $941.50, about 2 percent of salary; for the forty-year veteran, also with $50,000 in salary, the pension will be about 75 percent of his last year's salary, or $37,660 annually.

---

### FIGURE 8.1

### Private Employer Pension Formula

The participant receives credit equal to a percentage of earnings for each year of service: 1.25% of the first $7,800 and 2% thereafter. For the $50,000-a-year executive: $97.50 plus $844 for a total of $941.50. At age 65, after 20 years of employment: $18,830 annually. For those who continue to work after age 70½, the additional benefits will be reduced by the value of the regular pension payments.

When annual covered compensation in

| One Year Was | 1.25% of $7,800 | 2% Over $7,800 | Total Annual Benefit |
|---|---|---|---|
| $20,000 | 97.50 | $244.00 | $341.50 |
| 30,000 | 97.50 | 444.00 | 541.50 |
| 40,000 | 97.50 | 644.00 | 741.50 |
| 50,000 | 97.50 | 844.00 | 941.50 |

*Long-Term Employment*

| Average Annual Compensation | Years to Age 65 | Annual Retirement Benefit |
|---|---|---|
| $20,000 | 20 | $ 6,830 |
| | 30 | 10,245 |
| | 40 | 13,660 |
| $30,000 | 20 | $10,830 |
| | 30 | 16,246 |
| | 40 | 21,660 |
| $40,000 | 20 | $14,830 |
| | 30 | 22,245 |
| | 40 | 29,660 |
| $50,000 | 20 | $18,830 |
| | 30 | 28,245 |
| | 40 | 37,660 |

Remember: 1) IRS mandates withdrawal at age 70½ under a formula to complete payout during actuarial life expectancy; 2) reduced Social Security benefits for working from age 63–69.

## The Federal Employee Retirement System

Government employment is likely to provide benefits that are more generous than those of private industry. On average, the Federal Employees Retirement System, together with Social Security, pays about 60 percent of the last working year's salary for long-timers. This plan also encourages personal savings with modest matching. If you have five years of service and leave early, you may start to receive benefits at the age of sixty-two. One problem: federal pensions have annual cost of living adjustments lower than those of social security.

## State and Local Government Pensions

Historically, pensions on the state and local level have been similar to those of the federal government, with less paid for regular jobs, and more paid for police and fire fighters because of the dangers involved. Benefits generally reflect a higher percentage of working pay than is found in private industry, and the systems are likely to encourage early retirement.

## KEOGH AND PROFESSIONAL CORPORATION (PC) PENSION PLANS
...

Keogh and Professional Corporation (PC) plans are the oldest types of pension plans for small organizations, such as groups of physicians, dentists, lawyers, and architects. They enable long-time

---

### FIGURE 8.2

### Annual Pension Benefits Under Federal Employees Retirement System (FERS)

Mary, a clerical employee, retires at age 62 after 30 years of creditable service. Her last year's salary was $20,000; her final three-year average salary, $18,970. She worked five years outside the U.S. Civil Service. Her total Social Security coverage was 35 years. The example shows benefits with contributions to a Thrift Savings Plan: 2% annually. If Mary had saved the maximum of 5% of earnings, her pension would be about 10% greater.

|  | Dollars | Annual Pension % Final Salary |
|---|---|---|
| Social Security* | $ 4,840 | 24 |
| Payments: |  |  |
| 1.  1% × $18,970 × 30 years | 6,260 | 31 |
| Thrift Plan |  |  |
| 2.  2% of salary | 2,360 | 12 |
| Total | $13,460 | 67 |

If saved 5% of salary—$4,720—her total pension would be $15,820 or 79% of her last year's earnings.

---

* $4,150 attributed to federal service.

participants to accumulate substantial assets for retirement—as much as $1 million.

These "small" plans provide worthwhile tax advantages. For the employer, the contributions are deductible business expenses; for the employee, the allocations are not taxable income when paid, and the income and appreciation of the investments accumulate tax-deferred until withdrawal.

In recent years, Congress has tightened the rules to speed vesting and to minimize discrimination in favor of executives or owners. Another change has permitted employer contributions to be reduced by inclusion of a part of Social Security taxes. In addition, benefits have been limited by taxing withdrawals when accumulated assets rise above a set level.

Keoghs are concerned only with pensions; PC plans have advantages in other areas, such as company-paid life insurance, deferred compensation, and tax savings. Under recent rules, the pension provisions for both are similar. Contributions may be made up to $30,000 a year or 25 percent of compensation, whichever is less. With Keoghs, this percentage is net-after-contribution, so, with an annual salary of $100,000, the maximum contribution is $20,000—25 percent of $80,000.

Vesting (where participant is entitled to all contributions plus income/appreciation) is 20 percent after three years of service, 40 percent after four years, 60 percent after five years, 80 percent after six years, and 100 percent after seven years.

Keogh and PC plans may be either Defined Contribution Plans (DCPs) or Defined Benefit Plans (DBPs).

In a Defined Contribution Plan the annual allocations must be the same percentage of compensation for everyone. For example, when the trust agreement sets 10 percent, Nurse Nellie, who earns $24,000 a year, gets $2,400. Dr. Bruce, who earns $180,000 a year, gets $18,000.

In a Defined Benefit Plan, the retirement goal is the basis for actuarial calculations of the annual contributions needed. Typically, the actuary projects a 6 percent annual yield. If the assets grow faster than that, as they often do, the contributions in later years must be decreased to keep the overall fund on target. In 1990, plans were allowed total assets of $512,910 and annual retirement income of $102,582—both subject to indexing for inflation.

Both Keoghs and PCs can also use profit-sharing plans. No profits, no contributions. If there are profits, the contributions must be the same percentage of compensation for all participants, the lesser of $30,000 or 15 percent of compensation.

Under new rules, voluntary contributions count toward the $30,000 maximum, and the amount of salary that can be counted in the calculations is capped at $209,200 (adjusted annually for inflation). Thus, with a 10 percent formula plan plus profit-sharing, for the $300,000 a year physician, the $30,000 would drop to $20,920 (10 percent of $209,200) for the pension plan and $9,080 ($30,000 less $20,920) to the profit-sharing fund.

# JOINT PARTICIPATION PLANS
...

These are becoming more popular because they provide extra benefits: *for the employer,* savings since the annual contributions are not part of compensation; for the *employee,* the opportunity to determine the amount of savings, to benefit from matching contributions by the employer (typically, 10 to 50%), and to reduce current income taxes.

These plans can be worthwhile, but be sure to get full information from your Industrial Relations Department and, if substantial sums are involved, your tax adviser. Congress and the IRS keep changing the rules!

Here are the most widely used types:

## 401(k) Plans
Widely used because of its flexibility and simplicity. It allows the employee to take advantage of tax breaks via salary reduction, permits matching employer contributions, and is easy to administer, but its funding is limited: in 1990, the maximum, per-

employee contribution was $8,475 (to be indexed for future inflation).

Here's an example of how a 401(k) plan works. Justin earns $50,000 a year. He sets aside $3,500 in a 401(k), and his employer kicks in $2,500, or 5 percent of Justin's salary for a total of $6,000.

The immediate benefit comes in Justin's taxes. His gross income is reduced by $3,500, to $46,500, and he saves $980 on his income tax.

Then there's the retirement benefit. Let's assume that Justin and his employer keep socking away only $6,000 annually for the next twenty-five years and his account earns an average rate of return of 8 percent. Justin's nest egg will be $438,630. Even after the erosion of inflation, that can provide a welcome income.

## 403(b) Plans

A variation of the 401(k) designed for eligible employees of tax-exempt religious, charitable, or educational organizations. The maximum annual contribution is 20 percent of salary up to a limit of $9,500 (indexed for inflation). There are complicated rules for "includable compensation" and tax benefits and withdrawals, but when there's a job change, the balance can be transferred to another 403(b) plan or rolled over into an IRA.

## Simplified Employee Pension (SEP)

Popular with small business/professions (no more than twenty-five employees). It involves Individual Retirement Accounts under a company umbrella, requires a minimum of paperwork and permits contributions, per participant, up to 15 percent of compensation, to a maximum of $30,000 a year. Each employee owns his/her own fund and, generally, must be twenty-one years of age and have worked for the same firm for three of the last five years. SEPs may not be set up by state or local governments or tax-exempt organizations.

The company's contributions are deductible business expenses and are not included as taxable wages. If the employee

---

**FIGURE 8.3**

---

## Calculating Retirement Income from More than One Pension Plan

When several pension plans are involved, here's how to make projections:

Dustin, age 40, expects to work until age 70 . . . 30 more years. He accepts a better job with another company where he joins a 401(k) pension plan to which the annual contribution will be $4,000: $3,000 by Dustin, $1,000 by the employer.

Dustin leaves his vested pension assets of $30,000 in trust with the old firm. With both plans, he projects an annual rate of return of 8%. See Figure 6.2 for the factors in lines 4 and 7.

---

| | |
|---|---:|
| 1. Current value of existing pension plan | $30,000 |
| 2. Number of years to retirement | 30 |
| 3. Anticipated rate of investment return | 8% |
| 4. Growth factor, single-sum | 10.06 |
| 5. Value of these assets at age 70 (lines 1 × 4) | $301,800 |
| 6. Annual contribution to 401(k) | $4,000 |
| 7. Growth factor of 401(k) @ 8% after 30 years | 113.28 |
| 8. Value of assets at age 70 (lines 6 × 7) | $453,120 |
| 9. Total value of pension assets | $754,920 |

---

wishes, he or she can sign up for a salary reduction plan where the contribution, a current maximum of $8,475 annually, can be used to reduce the income tax base.

The system requires a minimum of paperwork. Administration is handled by one manager, such as a bank, an insurance company, or a mutual fund. There's a single annual report to the IRS, and each participant can direct where the savings are to be invested.

## Supplementary Employees Retirement Plan (SERP)

The SERP is a special format for highly compensated executives. At age sixty-five, the payout can be up to $102,582 (indexed for inflation). But there is no vesting, and there are no regular contributions. A SERP is only a promise. If long-term profits are low or the firm is taken over, the promise may evaporate. In special situations, however, SERPs can be useful tools.

## Sub-Chapter S Corporation

A format widely used by small, closely held businesses. As described by one tax adviser, "It looks like a corporation, and it smells like a corporation, but it is taxed like a partnership or a sole proprietorship." This means it avoids the double taxation of dividends that occurs with corporations—first the corporation gets to pay income tax on its profits, and then, when it declares a dividend and sends you a check, you get to pay taxes on the dividend.

Pension plans can be set up under standard rules but, with Defined Benefit Plans, because profits can be retained, annual contributions can be raised under a schedule based on age and compensation. The tax savings can be substantial because pension contributions are deductible business expenses and profits may be taxed at a lower rate than if the levies were paid as an individual shareholder.

There are disadvantages: taxes on profits over $150,000 a year; no more than 35 shareholders; one class of stocks; no borrowing; and, when passive income (money paid to a nonemployee shareholder) exceeds 25 percent of profits in three consecutive years, the company forfeits its special status. With knowledgeable counsel, the S format can make it possible for a $100,000-a-year executive to set aside up to $50,000 in a tax-deferred pension plan.

## FIGURE 8.4

### Programs for Tax-Deferred Savings

| Type Plan | Vesting | Participation | Annual Contributions | When Leave/Retire |
|---|---|---|---|---|
| IRA | Immediate | Individual with earned income | $2,000 single; $2,250 when non-working spouse | All assets |
| 401(k) 403(b) | Immediate | All eligible employees | Maximum of $8,475, can be matched by employer. Contribution can be deducted from salary to lower federal income tax. | All assets |
| SEP | Immediate | All eligible employees when 25 or fewer | To lesser of 15% of compensation or $30,000 a year. | In effect, this involves a series of IRAs under one management. |

| Keogh and Professional Corporation | 100% after three years' service or 20% annually to 100% after 7 years | All eligible employees | Same % of compensation for all employees to lesser of 25% or $30,000 with Defined Contribution Plan. | Vested assets only when leave early; at retirement, lump sum or annuity. |
| | | | With Defined Benefit Plan, actuary sets goal, then calculates savings needed. | Penalty of 15% on distributions in excess of $136,204 a year at age 70½. |

Note: Plans that set specific dollar limits will be adjusted for inflation, probably annually.

# A NOTE ON LOANS
...

With most pension plans it is possible to take out tax-free loans. Normally, when the vested assets are $20,000 or less, you can borrow up to 50 percent of total assets. When assets are more than $20,000, you can borrow half the savings up to $50,000—minus any outstanding loan balance of the previous twelve months.

For instance, if Dr. Tignor has $100,000 in a Keogh and a prior loan of $20,000, he can borrow $30,000 more. The interest rate must be competitive, and repayment must be made within five years, except when the money is used to buy a home. The interest paid is not tax-deductible.

# NINE

..........

# INDIVIDUAL RETIREMENT ACCOUNTS: STILL VALUABLE

The Individual Retirement Account is a do-it-yourself pension. Any individual with earned income can set one up. The maximum annual contribution is $2,000 for an individual, and $2,250 for a couple where one spouse doesn't work. All income and gains compound tax-deferred until withdrawal, generally permissible at age 59½, mandatory at 70½.

Originally, all of the savings were tax deductible on your federal income tax return, but in 1986, in an effort to raise revenues, Congress ruled that the contributions would be 100 percent deductible only if you were not covered by a company pension plan and your adjusted gross income (AGI) was less than $25,000 when single, or $40,000 when married and filing jointly. If income is over those amounts, the tax deduction is phased out at the rate of $200 for every $1,000 in income over the limit. (See Figure 9.1)

## Examples

Jack Hart is single, has an AGI of $26,000, and is not covered by a pension plan. He contributes $2,000 to his IRA each year.

### FIGURE 9.1

## Allowable Tax Deductions Under IRAs

| Filing Status | Adjusted Gross Income* | Allowable Deduction |
|---|---|---|
| Single | Up to $24,999 | Full amount to $2,000 |
| | $25,000–$34,999 | Deduction reduced by $200 for every $1,000 over $25,000 |
| Married/ joint filing | Up to $34,999 | Full amount to $2,000 or $2,250 when nonworking spouse |
| | Over $40,000 | Deduction reduced by $200 for every $1,000 over $40,000 |

* Adjusted Gross Income determined before reduction for any deductible contribution to IRA.

His tax deductible portion is $1,800. The calculation is as follows:

1. Excess of income above $25,000 = $1,000.
2. Subtract #1 from $10,000 = $9,000.
3. Multiply #2 by .20 (contribution of $2,000) = $1,800 deductible.

After Jack marries June, their AGI is $43,000 with a joint return. June is a participant in her employer's pension plan, so the maximum IRA is still Jack's $2,000. However, the deductible changes.

1. Excess of income above $40,000 = $3,000.
2. Subtract #1 from $10,000 = $7,000.
3. Multiply #2 by .20 = $1,400 deductible.

# Recommendations for IRAs
...

With the elimination of the full deduction in 1986, IRAs became less popular. Annual contributions dropped from $36 billion to less than $20 billion.

To rebuild interest and to encourage savings, there are several proposals to expand IRAs:

- An annual deduction on federal income tax of 50 percent of all contributions up to $2,000.
- Tax-free withdrawal of earnings on nondeductible savings after age 59½.
- No penalties for early withdrawals when the savings are used to purchase a first home, pay college costs of family members, or meet catastrophic medical expenses.
- Exclusion of taxes on 30 percent of capital gains of pension assets acquired after 1991 or on a portion of profits, to a maximum of 35 percent after seven years, depending on how long the assets are held.

---

### FIGURE 9.2

### Why IRAs Are Worthwhile

Some financial advisers argue that the tax deferral gained from IRAs is not worthwhile. That will be true over a short period but not for the long-term savings of a pension plan. Here's what happens with an annual investment of $2,000.

| For 10 years | Investment | Compounded Total | 28% Tax | Net |
|---|---|---|---|---|
| 7% tax-exempt bond fund | $20,000 | $ 27,640 | | $ 27,640 |
| 9% taxable bond fund | 20,000 | 30,400 | 8,512 | 21,888 |
| 9% IRA | 20,000 | 30,400 | | 30,400 |

| | | Compounded | | |
|---|---|---|---|---|
| For 20 years | Investment | Total | 28% Tax | Net |
| 7% tax-exempt bond fund | 40,000 | 80,200 | | 80,200 |
| 9% taxable bond fund | 40,000 | 102,400 | 28,672 | 73,728 |
| 9% IRA | 40,000 | 102,400 | | 102,400 |

FIGURE 9.2 (*continued*)

IRAs are a wise investment for almost everyone. If you move into a higher income tax bracket (not so rare these days), your real benefits will be even greater. Before the elimination of the full deduction, Americans invested $36 billion a year in IRAs. Today, those contributions are down 50 percent.

# IRA ROLLOVERS
...

These can be valuable when pension assets are withdrawn early. You take out your vested holdings and put them in an IRA where they remain tax-deferred until age 70½.

The rollover can be used to create a sort of portable pension when you change jobs, because you can freeze the original nest egg and start a second retirement plan with your new employer. It's also an excellent parking place with early retirement until you must start payouts.

The shift can be made once a year and can involve part or all of the vested assets. It must be completed within sixty days, and it must involve a shift from one plan to another (not yourself), or you will be subject to a 10 percent levy by the IRS and the immediate payment of taxes.

## Example
In a cost-cutting drive, BIGCO offers older employees early retirement on favorable terms. Vice president Vic, age sixty, chooses a

lump sum of $150,000, uses $50,000 to buy a small business, and rolls $100,000 into an IRA. At an annual rate of return of 8 percent, the fund will grow to $216,000 when he must start taking benefits, at age 70½. At that point Vic can either sell his new business and invest the proceeds, or he can keep going. At age seventy, Social Security's earnings test lapses, and he can collect full benefits while continuing to earn as much money as he wants.

## Caveats
When the IRA rollover involves large amounts of money, as is often the case when a departing executive receives a lump-sum payment from a corporate pension plan, proceed with care.

Be sure to name a beneficiary for your IRA rollover, and also, for flexibility, a series of heirs. You might want to set up a trust for the benefit of your spouse, children, and grandchildren. This setup gives each beneficiary the choice of taking the money or passing it on. Without a named beneficiary, the IRA assets will become part of your estate when you die, and will be subject to both income and estate taxes.

If you die after starting distribution at age 70½, the payments must be made to the heirs at least as quickly as called for in the original schedule. But in the event of death before age 70½, whether or not distributions have been made, you have choices: either a full payout by the end of the fifth year after death, or distribution in annual amounts over the life expectancy of the heir. Younger beneficiaries will obviously want to choose the second option. Payments may also be delayed until the end of the year the decedent would have turned 70½.

# TEN

.......

# OTHER TYPES OF SAVINGS FOR RETIREMENT

While pension plans are still the best way to go for most people, insurance companies offer a wide—and expanding—variety of policies designed to translate current savings into future benefits. These provide tax deferral and, after retirement, lifetime income and, in some cases, death benefits. They have proven so successful that a few firms are considering an all-purpose, once-a-month premium policy that will pay for a pension, life insurance, and some health care costs. Find out about these "opportunities" if you have, or can anticipate, extra savings. Here are some of the most useful ways to assure extra retirement income.

## ANNUITIES
...

Annuities are agreements with insurance companies that are supplements to, not substitutes for, pension plans. For an investment of $5,000 or more, the insurer guarantees to pay you and/or a

---

**FIGURE 10.1**

---

## Payouts on Two Annuities, Each Purchased for $10,000

**Retirement Assurance: 8.2% tax-deferred**

| Age at purchase | Annual lifetime income starting at age | | | |
|---|---|---|---|---|
|  | 70 | 75 | 80 | 85 |
| 45 | $9,774 | $19,279 | $40,456 | $101,738 |
| 50 | 6,426 | 12,342 | 26,292 | 65,794 |
| 55 | 4,143 | 8,002 | 16,903 | 41,968 |
| 60 | 2,706 | 5,075 | 10,516 | 26,311 |
| 65 | 1,771 | 3,248 | 6,487 | 15,800 |

**Fixed Retirement Annuity: 7.8% tax-deferred**

| Age at purchase | | | | |
|---|---|---|---|---|
| 45 | $7,884 | $13,205 | $23,290 | $ 41,244 |
| 50 | 5,336 | 9,071 | 15,672 | 28,332 |
| 55 | 3,665 | 6,139 | 10,767 | 19,068 |
| 60 | 2,518 | 4,217 | 7,287 | 13,104 |
| 65 | 1,729 | 2,897 | 5,004 | 8,856 |

*Source:* IDS Financial Corp.

beneficiary a fixed sum, usually every month, for life, generally starting at age sixty-five but, increasingly, at age seventy.

An annuity can be purchased at any age, with a single sum or by periodic savings. These dollars are not deductible on your federal income tax, but interest, dividends, and appreciation are tax-deferred until withdrawal. Acquisition costs and maintenance and severance fees are high, so buy one only when you plan to hold it for at least ten years.

1. Deal only with top-rated insurance companies—those licensed to do business in Connecticut, Massachusetts, New York, and Pennsylvania.

2. Shop several companies because terms, costs, and benefits vary widely.
3. Look for flexibility in amount and timing of the money you pay in—more when you get a bonus, less when there are unexpected bills.
4. Insist on a choice of investments, which can be either *fixed,* where funds are used to buy debt issues that pay returns of 7 to 8 percent guaranteed for a year or two, or *variable,* where holdings are partly in stocks whose incomes fluctuate and whose values (if things go well) will grow.
5. Compare all costs: commissions, deductions for early withdrawals, and mortality fees if you should live beyond actuarial years.

All payments are taxable until the annuity earnings have been distributed; thereafter, they are tax-free as a return of capital.

Annuities are *not* insured, and the insurance company *can* go bankrupt. However, most states have guarantee funds to reimburse policyholders if the underwriter is unable to do so.

## SINGLE PREMIUM
## LIFE INSURANCE (SPLI)
###### •••

Single premium life insurance is a first cousin to the annuity. It provides you with income while you're alive (you borrow from the cash value of the policy) and with tax advantages when you die (the proceeds go to beneficiaries free of income tax).

The initial investment should be substantial, at least $10,000. Preferably it should be paid in a single sum, but payments can be spread over several years. The loans are available only after payment of seven annual premiums.

### Example
Cyril, age 55, invests $100,000 in a seven-payment annuity combo with $17,422 used to pay the first seven premiums of a life

policy with an initial, guaranteed death benefit of $226,939. That $17,422 can be borrowed at the first anniversary date with the balance of $82,578 used to fund the annuity from which the next six premiums are paid.

---

**FIGURE 10.2**

---

**Single Premium Life Policy: $100,000**

| End of Year | Cash Value Insurance | Annuity | Death Benefit |
|:---:|:---:|:---:|:---:|
| 1 | $ 17,422 | $88,509 | $226,939 |
| 2 | 35,327 | 71,087 | 226,939 |
| 3 | 55,387 | 58,771 | 226,939 |
| 4 | 77,404 | 45,570 | 226,939 |
| 5 | 101,436 | 31,421 | 226,939 |
| 6 | 127,638 | 16,256 | 245,983 |
| 7 | 156,183 | 0 | 290,270 |

---

At age seventy-five, the death benefit would be over $539,000 and the cash value almost $398,000.

Each time the annuity fund makes an insurance payment, this represents a distribution to the annuity owner, partly taxable (20.5 percent) and partly a tax-free return of capital (79.5 percent).

With annual payments of $17,422, Cyril must include $3,572 in his gross income. In the 28 percent tax bracket, he pays a federal income tax of $1,000 while the policy is being paid for.

An SPLI policy can be a welcome supplement to Social Security and pension plan benefits. If you make this choice, do your homework first. Shop around, again deal only with an A (or better) rated insurance company, and have the agent review the contract, and all projections, line by line.

## POOLED INCOME PLAN (PIP)
•••

This is a special form of annuity based on a gift, in cash or property, to a qualified eleemosynary institution such as a college or hospital. The donor takes a tax deduction, based on age and tax bracket; the beneficiary pays an annual sum, usually in quarterly installments from the interest and dividends, to the donor and, often, to the spouse for as long as either lives. At the final death, the assets go to the institution.

Here's one university's program. The amount of the gift in this example is $10,000.

### Pooled Income Plan

| Age of donor | Annual payment (starting at age 65) | Charitable deduction in year of gift |
|---|---|---|
| 50 | $1,320 (13.2%) | $8,140 |
| 55 | $1,080 (10.8%) | $7,430 |
| 60 | $870 (8.7%) | $6,430 |

The best gift taxwise, is appreciated property—for instance, shares of stock now selling at 100 and bought, some years ago, at 25. At age sixty, if one hundred shares of this stock were sold, the capital gain would be $7,500 and the tax $2,100 or more. By giving away the shares, you get a tax credit of $6,430 and, at age sixty-five, lifetime income of as much as $870 a year.

## NEW LONG-LIFE POLICY
•••

The IRS requires that pension payouts be scheduled to be completed at the actuarial life expectancy of the beneficiary(ies). Since many people live longer, the checks stop when, often, they are most needed.

One way to protect yourself from this problem is to invest in a Retirement Assurance policy and arrange for its payouts to start after you receive the last check from your pension plan under the IRS withdrawal schedule. A Retirement Assurance policy is a combination of an annuity that provides a modest lifetime income with a tontine, the eighteenth-century lottery where the last survivor received a huge sum. With this type of policy, you can win a bundle when you outlive your peers.

## Example

Pomeroy, age forty-five, has a choice. With $10,000 he can buy a fixed annuity that will pay, at age seventy, $7,884 a year; at age seventy-five, $13,205 a year; at age eighty, $23,290 a year. Or he can buy a Retirement Assurance policy where the longer he waits to start withdrawals, the greater the benefits: at age eighty, $40,456 a year; at age eighty-five, a whopping $101,738 a year!

Pomeroy arranges for his regular pension, starting at age seventy, to be paid out over fifteen years, faster than the IRS-mandated minimum of 18.3 years. At age eighty-five, the Retirement Assurance policy takes over and starts paying more than $100,000 a year for as long as he and his spouse live!

# ELEVEN

..............

# RULES FOR WITHDRAWALS FROM RETIREMENT PROGRAMS

**W**ell before you retire, check with your tax adviser or the local office of the Internal Revenue Service to be sure that you understand the rules for pension payouts.

Generally, withdrawals before age 59½ are subject to a 10 percent penalty plus taxes unless made because of death or disability, to pay for catastrophic medical expenses (in excess of 7.5 percent of adjusted gross income), "hardship" as defined in the plan document or by naming a younger beneficiary. After age 70½, payouts must start and, in most cases, additional contributions are prohibited.

At the withdrawal date, you must choose between an immediate lump sum and an annuity with a minimum annual payment under IRS rules.

# LUMP SUM PAYOUT
•••

You can take all or part of the assets of the plan as a lump sum. Such a payout provides immediate cash and, when made with any type of plan except an IRA, can save taxes under five-year averaging. This choice permits the income taxes to be paid, in the year of withdrawal, as a single person with no exemptions—a rate about half that of the regular levy.

When the beneficiary is younger than seventy, he or she can shift the money into a rollover IRA so the savings will continue to grow tax-deferred. Figure 11.1 shows the difference between using an IRA rollover (#1) and using five-year averaging (#2). The beneficiary is a sixty-year-old female, and the pension sum is $200,000.

Both the rollover and the five-year averaging project approximately equal payments, in terms of spendable money, for her life expectancy of twenty-five years. The rollover provides higher annual distributions, but the taxes are more than double those of the five-year payout. In terms of spendable money, the rollover does come out a bit ahead.

For affluent retirees, the choice will probably be made on whether the bigger IRA payments push the beneficiary into a higher tax bracket.

With any type of lump sum distribution, high earners have to be careful because there's a 15 percent excise tax on withdrawals in excess of $136,204 a year (adjusted annually for inflation).

A major problem with lump sum distributions is that too many retirees are overwhelmed with the size of the payout and, instead of setting up an annuity to provide life-long income, splurge with an expensive vacation, the purchase of a dreamed-of luxury automobile, or simply by paying for a higher-than-justified life-style. All too soon, these dollars are gone and, with them, essential income. This is foolish and can lead to financial problems, restricted living, and psychological depression.

## FIGURE 11.1

### Lump Sum Distribution of $200,000 Pension Plan

Annual yield: 8%; income tax rate: 28%; payout; over 25 years

|  | #1: IRA Rollover Distribution | | Taxes | | #2: 5-Year Averaging Spendable Money | |
|---|---|---|---|---|---|---|
|  | #1 | #2 | #1 | #2 | #1 | #2 |
| **Annual Payout** | $ 17,348 | $ 13,497 | $ 4,857 | $ 2,037 | $ 12,491 | $ 11,460 |
| **Total** | $433,700 | $337,425 | $121,425 | $50,925 | $312,275 | $286,500 |

# Long-Term Distribution
...

When you make the decision on a long-term distribution, you must follow the IRS schedule, which is based on life expectancies. (See Figure 11.2 for a summary of the IRS schedule.)

---

**FIGURE 11.2**

---

## Joint Life Expectancy for
## Withdrawing Pension Assets

| Male Age | Female Same | (digested) Female Younger by | | | Female Older by | | |
|---|---|---|---|---|---|---|---|
| | | 1 | 3 | 5 | 1 | 2 | 3 |
| 59 | 26.9 | 27.4 | 28.5 | 29.6 | 26.4 | 25.9 | 25.4 |
| 60 | 26.0 | 26.5 | 27.6 | 28.8 | 25.5 | 25.1 | 24.6 |
| 62 | 24.4 | 24.9 | 25.9 | 27.1 | 23.9 | 23.5 | 23.0 |
| 65 | 22.0 | 22.5 | 23.5 | 24.6 | 21.6 | 21.1 | 20.7 |
| 67 | 20.5 | 21.0 | 21.9 | 23.0 | 20.1 | 19.6 | 19.2 |
| 70 | 18.3 | 18.3 | 19.7 | 21.2 | 17.9 | 17.5 | 17.1 |

*Source: Internal Revenue Service, Publication 575.*

To determine the minimum amount that must be withdrawn, divide the total assets by the appropriate life expectancy of both partners (unless the spouse signs away her/his right). Thus, when both Mr. and Mrs. Hopeful are age 70, their figure is 18.3. For a $100,000 fund: $5,464 a year. Meantime, the remaining assets continue to grow tax-deferred.

The annual payments can be more than those indicated by the IRS schedule, but never less. Here's how to use the table. Assume that Mr. and Mrs. Hopeful are both seventy years old. Their joint life expectancy is 18.3 years. Thus, with a $100,000 fund, the first-year payout must be at least $5,464 ($100,000 divided by 18.3). In year two, their joint life expectancy will be 17.3 years, so the divisor for the second year is 17.3, not 18.3.

Age makes a big difference in these calculations. If Mr. Hopeful is seventy, but Mrs. Hopeful is sixty-two, their joint life expectancy is 24.7 years (this figure is not on the summary table, but it is on the full IRS schedule). The first withdrawal is then $100,000 divided by 24.7, or $4,049. This is $1,415 less than when both Mr. and Mrs. Hopeful are seventy.

To prolong payouts, name a younger beneficiary—a nephew, perhaps. The maximum allowable age spread, except for a spouse, is ten years.

Early withdrawals are not subject to the 10 percent penalty when the payments are structured for substantially equal periodic payments keyed to life expectancy. Again, divide the life expectancies into the available dollars. If both spouses are fifty, the life expectancy is 33.1 years. If the nest egg is $100,000, the annual payment will be $3,021. After five years of payments, if you are

---

### FIGURE 11.3

### How Long Your Pension Payout Will Last

| Years | Rate of Return on Investment | | | | |
| | 8% | 9% | 10% | 12% | 15% |
|---|---|---|---|---|---|
| 10 | $ 8,242 | $ 7,894 | $ 7,567 | $6,970 | $6,198 |
| 15 | 10,464 | 9,860 | 9,306 | 8,332 | 7,145 |
| 20 | 11,955 | 11,114 | 10,362 | 9,082 | 7,594 |
| 25 | 12,956 | 11,916 | 11,005 | 9,495 | 7,807 |
| 30 | 12,628 | 12,428 | 11,395 | 9,722 | 7,909 |

1. Start with the number of years you plan to draw on savings and the anticipated annual rate of investment return. The intersection shows the assets needed to draw $100 per month.
2. Divide the nest egg by that amount.
3. Multiply by 100 to determine the monthly amount.
*Example.* At age 65, Horatio has $100,000 in his at-work pension plan. His bride is 64, so their actuarial life span is about 22 years. They decide on a 20-year payout (faster than mandated by IRS) and assume a 10% average yield. These figures cross at $10,362.

They divide their $100,000 by $10,362 to get $965 monthly withdrawals: $11,580 a year.

To figure out how much capital is needed to yield $100 a month, find where the rate of return and years cross: at 9%, for 25 years: $11,916. To withdraw $1,000 a month ($12,000 annually), you will need 10 times that amount: $119,160.

still under age 59½, you have the option of stopping the with-drawals and adding to the savings until you're 59½.

To provide a base for projections, Figure 11.4 shows a systematic withdrawal plan from a mutual fund. The original investment, via an IRA rollover, is $100,000 in one thousand shares of a mutual fund yielding 10 percent annually. The payouts start low—$6,356—gradually rise to $11,497 when capital is invaded, and after year 13 they rise above $20,000 annually. The total payout is $248,087—$148,087 more than the original investment. This example is a good reason to choose an annuity over a lump sum payment.

# HOW MUCH OF YOUR PENSION WILL BE TAX-FREE?
...

When all of the assets in your pension plan represent contributions that were deductible business expenses (typically, when paid by the employer), the payouts are taxable income. But when you made voluntary contributions with after-tax dollars, the withdrawals will be tax-free because you already paid the taxes.

Figure 11.5 shows an IRA that included both deductible and voluntary savings. To calculate the sums that are taxable income, divide the total by the amount of tax-free savings. Here, 27 percent of the withdrawals are not subject to income tax, and 73 percent are taxable. So when you withdraw $5,000, you pay a tax, at 28 percent, on $3,650. To be sure that you make accurate calculations, consult a tax adviser.

For more information, get a copy of IRS Publication 17: *Your Federal Income Tax.* Employees of the U.S. Civil Service should get Publication 721 or call 1-800-829-3676.

## Check State Laws
If you worked for a state or local government, you may have to pay a tax on any pension or annuity income that originates within

# FIGURE 11.4

## Systematic Withdrawal Plan: Mutual Fund—16 Years

Original investment of $100,000 in 1,000 shares of mutual fund yielding 10% annually

| At the end of Year One | Income from Investments (A) | Amount added to * or withdrawn † from principal (B) | Total Payout (C) | Value of Shares |
|---|---|---|---|---|
| 1 | $ 10,007 | $ 3,651* | $ 6,356 | $103,600 |
| 2 | 10,347 | 3,331* | 7,016 | 106,900 |
| 3 | 10,650 | 2,906* | 7,745 | 109,800 |
| 4 | 10,904 | 2,356* | 8,549 | 112,000 |
| 5 | 11,007 | 1,661* | 9,436 | 113,900 |
| 6 | 11,212 | 796* | 10,416 | 114,600 |
| 7 | 11,230 | 266† | 11,497 | 114,400 |
| 8 | 11,133 | 1,558† | 12,690 | 112,800 |
| 9 | 10,893 | 3,115† | 14,008 | 109,700 |
| 10 | 10,484 | 4,978† | 15,462 | 104,700 |
| 11 | 9,873 | 7,194† | 17,067 | 97,500 |
| 12 | 9,022 | 9,817† | 18,839 | 87,700 |
| 13 | 7,888 | 12,907† | 20,795 | 74,800 |

| | | | | |
|---|---|---|---|---|
| 14 | 6,421 | 16,533† | 22,953 | 58,300 |
| 15 | 4,564 | 20,772† | 25,336 | 27,500 |
| 16 | 2,253 | 25,713† | 27,966 | 11,800 |
| Final | 111 | 11,845† | 11,956 | — |
| Total | 148,089 | 99,998 | 248,087 | — |

*Source:* Adapted from T. Rowe Price Associates.

* In the first six years of this example, the amount earned each year is split between an addition to the total payout and the balance, which is added to the value of the shares.

† In the remaining years, the amounts withdrawn come from both the earnings and the principal and are subtracted from the value of the shares.

Note: Column A plus/minus Column B = Column C.

---

**FIGURE 11.5**

---

## Withdrawals when Pension Plan Includes Both Deductible and Nondeductible Contributions

| Year | Savings Deductible | Nondeductible |
|------|-------------------|---------------|
| 1 | $2,000 | $ 0 |
| 2 | 2,000 | 0 |
| 3 | 2,000 | 0 |
| 4 | 1,000 | 1,000 |
| 5 | 1,000 | 1,000 |
| 6 | 0 | 2,000 |
| 7 | 0 | 2,000 |
| Total | $8,000 | $6,000 |

---

At retirement, the IRA is worth $22,500. You withdraw $5,000: $1,350 tax free; $3,650 taxable. Here's the arithmetic:

> Total assets: $22,500
> % tax-free: $6,000 / $22,500 = 27%
> Tax-free withdrawal: 27% × $5,000 = $1,350
> Taxable withdrawal: $5,000 − $1,350 = $3,650
> In 28% tax bracket, the tax is $1,022 to net $2,628
>     plus $1,350 tax-free = $3,978.

that state *even if you retire to another state.* The regulations do vary from state to state, so be sure to check out your individual situation. Among the states that have such a tax are California, Iowa, Kansas, Massachusetts, and New York. Arizona, Colorado, Nevada, and Utah also have such laws but do not enforce them at this time.

# TWELVE

......

# INVESTMENT STRATEGIES: QUALITY FIRST

In managing investments, whether personal or fiduciary, a few choices must be made at the very outset.

1. To invest for growth or for income, or for a combination of the two. Once that choice has been made:
2. To determine the allocations, overall and within each category, on the basis of the sleep-well level of you and your spouse. If either of you toss and turn when the price of your securities drops a few points, concentrate on *fixed* investments—those that provide *fixed* income for steady checks; those with *fixed* assets so that your principal will be returned at maturity.
3. To decide whether you will manage the portfolio or turn the responsibility over to someone else—a professional money manager or a mutual fund.

When you have the time and are willing to do your homework, you will make more money, and have more fun, by being your own manager. But, to continue to be successful, you must set strict rules and stick to them!

With pension savings, always recognize that these are fiduciary funds that should never be placed at risk. That means that if you have any qualms about any potential holdings, DON'T. There are always safe, rewarding opportunities, such as U.S. government bonds and the shares of the *quality* corporations that are the backbone of American business.

The number one criterion for investments of all types is QUALITY: the corporate record of financial strength, profitability, growth, and investment acceptance. This means a company that has ample assets and able management, that continues to make more and more money; and whose shares are widely owned by major investors such as mutual funds, insurance companies, and large pension plans.

---

## FIGURE 12.1

### Minimum Quality Ratings for Investments

**Investment Acceptance**

| Market Value | Trading Volume | Institutional Investors | Shareholders |
|---|---|---|---|
| $100 million | $50 million | 15 | 1,000 |

**Financial Strength**

| Capital/Surplus | Long Term Debt as % Capital | Working Capital Ratio |
|---|---|---|
| $50 million | Maximum: 50% | 2:1 (with exceptions for banks/utilities) |

**Profitability/Stability**

| 10-Year Average | Stability vs. Market | Dividend/Revenues Payout | |
|---|---|---|---|
| 11% | 60% | 10%–75% | No significant decline in one year |

**Growth**

| Annual Rate:<br>10 Years | Book Value<br>Per Share | Sales/Revenues<br>Per Share |
|---|---|---|
| +6% | +6% | +6% |

*Source:* Wright Investors' Service

Quality corporations are established organizations with a market value of $100 million, owned by 1,000 shareholders, of which at least 15 are institutions or funds. They have capital of $50 million, modest debt (less than 50% of capital), and working capital twice debt (except for utilities and financial institutions).

They must be well managed as proven by 10-year records: a return on equity (what shareholders own) of 11% or more, with no significant decline in more than one year and, usually, paying dividends of from 10% to 75% of profits.

Growth is essential: for a decade, +6% average annual rate for revenues/sales and book value.

Note: Quality corporations always have proven records of superior performance. That's why, over time, their shares will always be worth more!

To find quality companies, do your homework. Read financial reports, get research studies from your broker, check value line studies, watch the financial press, and use common sense. Once you have made a choice, be patient. Most worthwhile profits take at least twenty-four months. And, over time, more money can be made, with less risk, by investing in quality stocks than with any other types of securities.

Quality is essential with fiduciary funds, such as pension plans. These savings should *never* be put into deals on the basis of hopes, not facts; of promises, not performance; of tips, not research.

True investors buy quality stocks, preferably when they are undervalued, and sell them when they become fully priced. They know that, over the long term, they will make money from modest, growing dividends and substantial price appreciation. With the exception of stable utilities, quality corporations will boost their earnings by about 10 percent annually, pay out 25 to 50 percent of their profits in dividends, and invest the balance in new markets, more modern equipment, and research and development for continued growth. Such superior results attract more investors, and this demand raises the prices of their stocks.

Even greater profits can be achieved by managing the portfolio: by timing your buying and selling, and by shifting to bonds in down markets and moving back to stocks in up periods.

A good place to start your search for quality is with companies rated A or higher by Standard & Poor's. This stock guide is available from your broker and at your library.

Few of these firms will be glamorous, but they will be blue chips. Some will be large, most of medium size. A handful will be small—under $100 million a year in revenues. The majority will be companies that have grown slowly and steadily, with occasional spurts due to new products or acquisitions.

Figure 12.2 lists five major corporations that were quality companies in 1980 and continued such ratings in 1990. The utility (Central & Southwest) is included to show that income securities can pay off over time. Their growth will be slow and, usually, steady, and with a quality company the dividend will keep rising.

If you had bought one hundred shares of each of these companies for your pension plan in 1980, you would have invested $11,000. By 1990, those holdings would have grown to one 1,600 shares worth $95,798, and you would have received some $16,482 in dividends.

## SPECIAL TYPES OF STOCKS
•••

Within the stock categories, investments can be broken down further according to specific needs or goals. Such classification can be more important with personal portfolios than with pension plans because of the tax consequences. For instance, a moving-up executive who receives a sizable bonus will want to keep invest-

## FIGURE 12.2

### Quality Companies and How Their Shares Fared: 1980–1990

| Company | 1980 Shares | 1980 Cost | 1990 Shares | 1990 Value | Dividends 1980–1990 | Total Return |
|---|---|---|---|---|---|---|
| AMP, Inc. | 100 | $ 3,300 | 300 | $16,500 | $ 2,472 | $ 18,972 |
| American Home Prods. | 100 | 1,100 | 200 | 11,000 | 3,194 | 14,194 |
| Coca-Cola | 100 | 1,100 | 600 | 28,800 | 3,750 | 32,550 |
| Central & Southwest | 100 | 1,100 | 100 | 4,300 | 2,268 | 6,568 |
| General Electric | 100 | 4,400 | 400 | 35,198 | 4,798 | 35,198 |
| Totals | 500 | $11,000 | 1,600 | $95,798 | $16,482 | $107,482 |

*Source:* Wright Investors' Service.

## FIGURE 12.3

## Quality Corporations That Pay No/Low Dividends

| Company | Dividend | Average Earnings Increase: 1981–1990 | Earnings 1990 | Earnings 1996* | 1985 | Stock Price 1991 | Stock Price 1995* |
|---|---|---|---|---|---|---|---|
| Computer Sciences | No | + 8% | $4.22 | $9.70 | 13 | 67 | 133–107 |
| Crown Cork & Seal | No | + 8 | 3.58 | 8.28 | 15 | 69 | 139–116 |
| FlightSafety | 0.5 | +18 | 2.22 | 6.21 | 13 | 52 | 140–112 |
| Hewlett-Packard | 1.0 | +11 | 3.06 | 6.55 | 29 | 52 | 120–100 |
| Nordstrom, Inc. | 1.1 | +17 | 1.42 | 3.38 | 7 | 37 | 78–63 |
| Stryker Corp. | No | +21 | 1.00 | 2.84 | 5 | 40 | 78–63 |
| Toys "R" Us | No | +26 | 1.11 | 3.63 | 7 | 30 | 77–62 |
| Wal-Mart Stores | 0.5 | +37 | 1.14 | 4.32 | 5 | 40 | 115–96 |

*Source:* Wright Investors' Service.
* Estimated.

ment income at a minimum by buying shares of quality corporations that pay low or no dividends. See Figure 12.3.

For those who prefer income, stability, and slow growth, Figure 12.4 lists some current high dividends payers.

---

**FIGURE 12.4**

---

**Quality Companies with High Dividend Yields**

| Company | Yield | Return on Equity 1981–1990 | Earnings Growth 1981–1990 | Stock Price 1991 | Stock Price 1996* |
|---|---|---|---|---|---|
| Central & S.W. | 6.5% | 14.8% | +4% | 45 | 67–59 |
| First Union Bank | 5.9 | 16.8 | +7 | 22 | 42–36 |
| Florida Progress | 7.0 | 14.6 | +8 | 40 | 58–51 |
| Keycorp | 5.3 | 14.9 | +9 | 36 | 56–47 |
| Society Corp. | 5.1 | 14.5 | +9 | 39 | 69–59 |
| So. Indiana Gas | 6.3 | 15.3 | +6 | 33 | 47–42 |
| TECO Energy | 5.3 | 14.9 | +5 | 33 | 48–42 |
| Wisconsin P.S. | 7.0 | 14.4 | +3 | 24 | 37–32 |

*Source:* Wright Investors' Service.
* Estimated.

---

For a broader list, Figure 12.5 shows some quality companies with long records of profitable growth—returns on equity of about 20 percent a year or better, annual earnings gains generally of 10 percent or more, and rising dividends. The result, over the ten years 1981–1990, was capital appreciation between six- and tenfold!

This table is here to show all types of serious investors what quality looks like. Standard & Poor's rates all of these companies B+ or higher. However, these companies are listed here as examples, not recommendations. Use these companies as the basis for your own research. Find companies that *you* like, buy shares for

## FIGURE 12.5

### Quality Companies With Records of Profitable Growth

| Company | S&P Rating | Return on Equity 1981–1990 | Annual Earnings 1981–1990 | Earnings 1980 | Earnings 1990 | Stock Prices 1980–1991 Low | High | Recent |
|---|---|---|---|---|---|---|---|---|
| AMP, Inc. | A– | 19.8% | + 8% | $1.22 | $2.70 | 11 | 72 | 53 |
| Anheuser-Busch | A+ | 22.9 | +17 | .63 | 2.96 | 3½ | 53 | 27 |
| Bristol-Myers | A+ | 24.5 | +13 | 1.02 | 3.33 | 7½ | 80 | 78 |
| DeLuxe Corp. | A+ | 30.4 | +15 | .49 | 2.03 | 4½ | 42 | 37 |
| Emerson Electric | A+ | 19.8 | + 8 | 1.25 | 2.77 | 9½ | 45 | 44 |
| General Electric | A+ | 19.5 | +11 | 1.66 | 4.85 | 11 | 76 | 69 |
| General Mills | A | 25.8 | +10 | .96 | 2.78 | 7 | 61 | 57 |
| Giant Foods | A | 24.3 | +23 | .25 | 2.01 | 1 | 36 | 29 |
| Kellogg Company | A+ | 34.5 | +13 | 1.21 | 4.16 | 7½ | 95 | 92 |
| Melville Corp. | A+ | 23.3 | +12 | 1.14 | 3.59 | 6 | 58 | 53 |
| Wal-Mart Stores | A+ | 35.3 | +37 | .05 | 1.14 | 1 | 40 | 38 |

*Source:* Wright Investors' Service.

the long term, and review progress and prospects every six months.

Above all, remember that stocks *can* go down. Blue chips don't always continue to be blue chips. Twenty years ago, some of the firms that would have made a list of quality stocks were Avon Products, Falstaff Brewing, Firestone Tire, W. T. Grant, Howard Johnson, Petrolane, Ronson, and Sprague Electric. Avon is the only one of these companies that still exists under its old name, and it is no longer rated as a quality investment.

# THIRTEEN

......................

# BALANCING YOUR INVESTMENTS

The makeup of your personal and fiduciary portfolios should be planned according to your objectives, resources, risk tolerance, and time available for management. If you turn your assets over to someone else, directly or through mutual funds, the allocations will be broader than those of personal holdings, but the criteria should be similar. At all times, be comfortable. Look for rewarding but not super returns and, with your pension savings, safety and future income.

In almost all portfolios, there should be investments in debt securities with the timing and amount to be determined by your (and spouse's) sleep-well level, need for income, diversification, and economic/market conditions. With pension savings, your goal should be sure, ample assets at retirement:

- *To preserve capital* you should invest in fixed assets such as savings accounts, certificates of deposit, and money market funds.
- *To provide income and, often, capital appreciation* you should

invest in fixed income holdings such as bonds (taxable and tax-exempt) and packages of mortgages.

Most debt investments are safe. Savings accounts are insured up to $100,000. The bills, notes, and bonds issued or guaranteed by the U.S. Treasury are the best you can buy. The bonds and commercial paper of quality corporations, institutions, and governments are sure to pay interest and be redeemed at maturity.

Once again, the operative word is quality. In recent years, the phenomenon of junk bonds has reinforced the lesson. These are high-yield loans, secured by shaky assets and used primarily by promoters of takeovers. Even if the borrowers don't go bankrupt, the prices of these bonds will falter. It's too early to know if they will be redeemed at maturity.

Here are the most popular and useful types of debt investments:

## Money Market Funds

These are available from brokers, financial institutions, and mutual funds for $1,000 and up. They invest in liquid assets such as Treasury bills and notes, certificates of deposit, commercial paper, etc. They pay daily interest that is compounded, permit sales or purchases at net asset value, and charge management fees that appear modest but can add up to profitable sums for management. Their yields move with interest rates on short-term Treasuries and have ranged from more than 15 percent in the early 1980s to 7.5 percent recently.

These are convenient parking places for cash reserves while you are waiting for profitable investment opportunities. As your savings grow, arrange for these dollars to be tied in with your brokerage account so that all income will be swept into the fund quickly to keep earning interest.

## Certificates of Deposit (CDs)

These are available from banks and thrift institutions. They pay daily interest, compounded, but should be held to maturity, usu-

## FIGURE 13.1

### Risks and Returns of Fixed Asset/Income Investments

| Type | Risks of Change Value | Yield | Liquidity | Recent Yield | What to Check/Understand |
|------|-------|-------|-----------|--------------|--------------------------|
| Passbook Account | None | Minimal | High | 5% | May require minimum balance: check terms of compounding, additions, withdrawals. |
| NOW Accounts | None | Minimal | Medium | 5% | Any restrictions on check writing. |
| Money Market Funds: Bank | Low | Low | High | 5.55% | In rising markets, yields may be raised slowly. |
| Mutual Fund taxable | Low | Small shifts | High | 7.48% | Rates move with cost of money: look for short maturities of debt of quality borrowers with minimum of foreign loans. |
| tax-exempt | Low | Low | Medium | 5.20% | Rates change slowly: insist on A rating holdings. |

| | | | | | |
|---|---|---|---|---|---|
| Treasury Bills | | | | | |
| 1 year | Small | None | Medium | 7.54% | Interest exempt from state/local taxes. |
| Certificates of Deposit (CDs) | | | | | |
| 1 year | None | None | Fair | 8.45% | When compounded: 8.82% and 9%. Returns fluctuate so check before setting time. |
| 5 year | | | | 8.50% | |
| EE Savings Bonds | None | None | Low | 7.01% | Interest is 85% that of 5-year Treasuries with 6% minimum; interest free of state/local taxes. |

ally between six months and three years. Early withdrawals are subject to penalties, generally the loss of one to three months' interest.

## U.S. Savings Bonds

Series EEs sell at 50 percent of face value—$12.50 for a $25 bond. They earn 6 percent or 85 percent of the average yield of five-year Treasury notes and bonds. The interest accumulates tax-free and can be deferred by swapping for HH bonds, which pay 7.5 percent semiannually, with the interest taxable by the federal government but not by state and local authorities.

## U.S. Treasury Bills, better known as T-bills

These are available with maturities of 90 and 180 days and one year, at a minimum face value of $10,000. They are sold at a discount, so a one-year bill, with an 8 percent coupon, costs $9,200 for an actual yield of 8.7 percent. They can be bought directly from a Federal Reserve Bank or through a bank or broker.

## U.S. Treasury Notes

Available at $1,000 and up, with maturities up to three years, they're useful for temporary holdings while you decide on long-term investments.

## Straight Debt of the U.S. Government and Major Corporations

Except in times of high interest rates, these investments are better for pension plans than for personal portfolios. In small lots, their purchase involves hefty commissions. U.S. Treasuries are always the best, but you can get a slightly higher return with corporate debt. Always stick with issues of corporations that are rated Baa of BBB or higher by the credit rating services. Here's a list of the ratings used by the two major services.

|                   | Moody's | Standard & Poor's |
| ----------------- | ------- | ----------------- |
| Highest quality   | Aaa     | AAA               |
| High quality      | Aa      | AA                |
| Upper medium      | A       | A                 |
| Medium            | Baa     | BBB               |
| Speculative       | Ba      | BB                |

## Zero Coupon Bonds

Specialized debt instruments that are sold at far below face value, pay no interest, and are redeemed at par at a specified date, usually ten to thirty years from issue. The annual appreciation works out to an average rate of return that is higher than that of straight bonds. For example, a $1,000 zero with a twenty-year maturity might sell originally for $172. After ten years it will trade around $415, and at maturity it will be paid off at par: $1,000.

Zeros are excellent for pension funds but *not* suitable for personal portfolios because of the tax consequences. Even though there is no actual cash payout, the IRS and some states and local governments levy an income tax on the *imputed interest:* the annual increase in value of the security. That's all right with pension plans, where the taxes are deferred until withdrawal, but it can be costly and annoying for individual investors. (The appreciations of municipal zeros is exempt from federal taxes and local levies when the bonds are issued in your home state.)

The U.S. Treasury issues zero coupon bonds that are packaged by brokerage firms as STRIPS (Separate Trading of Registered Interest and Principal of Securities), CATs (Certificates of Treasury), and TIGERS (Treasury Investment Growth Receipts).

Other government entities and corporations also issue zero coupon bonds when they have an immediate need for cash and anticipate that the money can be used profitably, so that there will be sufficient funds for redemption at maturity.

GAINS (Growth and Income Securities) are special zeros that

turn into straight bonds after several years. Here's an example of
how this works. A $5,000 zero coupon bond, with a yield of 9.55
percent, costs $1,632. After 12½ years, it will be converted into
a regular bond paying the same rate of interest for another fifteen
years, to maturity. This is a good deal when used with a pension
plan. At retirement it can be converted to provide ample income,
possibly for life.

*With all zeros, be sure that there's an A in the rating.*

## Municipal Bonds

Debt of state, county, and local governments and agencies. The
interest is free of federal income taxes and of state and local levies
when the issuer is located in the state of residence of the investor.
Municipals are suitable for personal portfolios, but not for pension
plans, where the taxes are already deferred. Your best best: tax-
exempts that are insured by a consortium of insurance companies
to achieve a rating of A or better.

## Special Note

Almost all of these debt instruments are available through shares
of mutual funds, which we'll discuss in the next chapter. Mutual
funds give you the added advantage of automatic reinvestment of
interest for *compounding*.

# Mortgage-Backed Instruments
...

Another type of debt, with special appeal for older folks, is the
mortgage-backed security. Such securities are packages of debt on
buildings. The interest, amortization, and repayment of the
underlying debt are passed through to investors (after the sponsors
have taken their fees). These instruments pay comparatively high
yields, often over 10 percent, and can be bought directly, in units
of $25,000, or through shares of mutual funds, where the mini-
mum investment is usually $1,000. If you purchase them directly,

be prepared to hold them for a long time, because there may not be an active market for resale.

**Ginnie Maes** (Government National Mortgage Association) are pools of home loans insured by Uncle Sam and guaranteed by the Federal Housing Association or Veteran's Administration.

The investor receives a share of the payments of monthly interest and amortization. When there is a repayment or refinancing, he also gets a portion of these dollars. Most of the mortgages are for thirty years, but with repayments, the average life of a pool is fifteen years. That's why these pass-throughs should be bought primarily for pension funds or by individuals over the age of seventy with limited life expectancies. If the investor is younger, he or she may outlive the payouts.

**Freddie Mac** bonds are backed by fifteen-year mortgages bought by the Federal Home Loan Mortgage Corporation from the original lenders, usually thrift associations. The loans are packaged, with the covering certificates sold to investors.

**Fannie Maes** are pools of home loans sponsored by the Federal National Mortgage Association. The minimum units are $25,000.

Ginnie, Freddie, and Fannie all offer the investor a safe investment with a competitive yield and are suitable for most personal and pension portfolios, either directly or through shares of mutual funds. But their market values will fluctuate with the cost of money. For example, a 9.5 percent bond, bought at par, will decline in price when the interest rate rises to 11 percent.

**Collateralized Mortgage Obligations (CMOs)** are private Ginnie Maes, backed by home loans made by the issuing financial institutions. The yields are higher than those of government-backed loans, but be cautious. There is no way the investor can know the true value of the underlying properties. With one major bank, the loans were based on half-empty condominiums.

# CAVEAT
···

Generally, most investors buy debt issues as a base—for steady income, for stability, and for preservation of capital. These goals *may* be obtained over the years, but in the interim there can be significant shifts with changes in the cost of money. This means, if you have to sell, you may lose money. And those redemption dollars will be worth less because of inflation. Look at the record.

Between 1945 and 1965, the Dow-Jones bond average yields ranged from 1.9 percent to 4.6 percent. In the next ten years, they moved up to 9.2 percent, staying in that range until 1980, when they soared to 12 percent. They held high for the next five years and then declined slowly to 9.7 percent by 1990.

With all debt, the price moves opposite to the interest rate: *up* when it drops; *down* when it rises. Thus, Patriotic Peter, who bought twenty-year bonds in 1945 with a 1.9 percent coupon (interest of $190 per $1,000) would have had a paper loss for most of that period. If Peter, Jr., bought new twenty-year bonds in 1965, the yield would have been a comparatively welcome 4.6 percent. *But,* by 1980, with new issues paying 12 percent, their market value was below $400.

Joy finally came in the 1980s, when a twenty-year bond carried a 14 percent coupon. By 1990, if the issue had not been called, it would be selling at about $1,400!

Debt investments can be safe but not always rewarding. The only sureties are regular interest payments and full value at maturity. Always project future prices under changing interest rates and probable conditions when you get back your investment.

# CHECKPOINTS
···

- *Buy backwards.* Select the future dates when you will need money, and find bonds that mature at that time.
- *Choose medium-term debt*—due in ten or fifteen years. The values

of these issues will fluctuate less than those of instruments with shorter or longer maturities.

- *With less than $25,000,* buy shares of mutual funds. With larger investments, consult a knowledgeable broker or investment adviser. Some bonds have special provisions that mandate early redemption or permit exchanges that you may not like. Some tax-exempt issues allow the money to be used for purposes other than those outlined in the prospectus.
- *Avoid all trick deals.* Insist on quality, because you want to be sure that you will receive regular interest payments on time and face value at redemption.

## FIGURE 13.2

### How Inflation and Taxes Can Reduce a $250,000 Nest Egg to Zero in 7 Years

These projections are based on data from Peter Dickinson, famed author/lecturer on aging. They assume: average annual profit on stocks: +9%; total savings: $250,000; annual spending (in today's dollars): $25,000; Social Security COLAs: +3% a year; increased spending: +19%; inflation loss: +19%; tax bite: 25%.

We do not agree fully with Peter's dire projections but his conclusions point out the problems of older Americans and why it is so important for younger workers to build their own retirement assets.

| | Year 1 | Year 2 | Year 3 | Year 4 | Year 5 | Year 6 | Year 7 |
|---|---|---|---|---|---|---|---|
| Investment Profits | $ 22,500 | $ 20,045 | $ 17,343 | $ 14,318 | $10,907 | $ 7,019 | $ 2,552 |
| Social Security | 15,600 | 16,068 | 16,550 | 17,046 | 17,557 | 18,084 | 18,626 |
| Your Spending | 25,000 | 29,756 | 35,402 | 42,128 | 50,132 | 59,657 | 70,992 |
| Inflation Loss | 34,700 | 30,941 | 26,780 | 22,114 | 16,845 | 10,841 | 3,962 |
| Taxes | 5,625 | 5,011 | 4,335 | 3,580 | 2,727 | 1,755 | 638 |
| Nest Egg | $222,725 | $193,130 | $160,506 | $123,950 | $82,718 | $35,568 | below zero |

......................

# FOURTEEN

# WHAT YOU SHOULD KNOW ABOUT MUTUAL FUNDS

The most widely used form of securities investments are shares of mutual funds. These are pooled holdings managed by professionals for a wide variety of goals. Their shares, which represent the underlying assets, are sold to the public, usually at Net Asset Value (NAV) but, with Closed-End Funds, on a competitive basis of supply and demand.

Most management firms sponsor a group of funds and make it easy to switch—from growth to income in a down market; from debt to equity in a bull market. In addition to "professional" management of your assets, you get regular reports (valuable for tax purposes), can add or withdraw funds, can get up-to-date information on taxes, and can arrange for the custody and management of pension plans. But you will lose the fun of building your own wealth.

Broadly speaking, stock mutual funds can be classified by their methods of selling and investing.

**Load Funds** are sold through brokers, dealers, and special representatives. These sales persons receive a commission, ranging from 8.5 percent for the investment of small savings down to 2 percent for large commitments. The fee is taken off the top, so that less of your money actually goes to work. With an 8.5 percent load, only $91.50 of every $100 is invested. (If you figure the commission on the basis of what is actually invested, the commission rate is 9.29 percent—$8.50 divided by $91.50, and not $8.50 divided by $100.) But the sales person handles all details.

**No-Load Funds** are bought directly from the sponsoring firm without commission. All of your money is invested, but you must handle the mechanics—setting up the account, mailing checks, arranging for income to be reinvested or paid to you.

Both load and no-load funds are bought at net asset value—the market price of the underlying securities.

Look for a management firm that controls a number of funds with different objectives, so that it will be easy and inexpensive for you to shift types of investments.

Charges vary widely. Be sure to find out about the following:

- *Management fee.* Usually about 0.5 percent of assets. Be wary when it's more than 1.5 percent.
- *Back-end load (deferred sales levy).* This may be deducted from the proceeds of the sale of shares. Such charges typically run 4 to 6 percent for withdrawals in the first year and gradually decline to zero in year five.
- *Reinvestment fees.* These may be as much as 1.25 percent, so your 10 percent yield, when reinvested, may shrink to 8.75 percent.
- *Marketing costs.* Look for the telltale "12(b)-1" in the prospectus. This pays for expenses such as promotional literature and may include a "trailing commission"—extra compensation to the broker who sold the shares originally. Marketing costs can run from 0.3 percent to 2 percent of your money.

In an attempt to protect the consumer, the Securities and Exchange Commission now requires that the prospectuses of all mutual funds include a table disclosing the costs involved with a $1,000 investment over one, three, five, and ten years, assuming a 5 percent annual rate of return.

With some two thousand American mutual funds (and a growing number that concentrate on foreign holdings) there are choices to fit every purse and objective. Take your time in making a decision, and do not hesitate to make a change, after a reasonable period, if you are not happy with the service. Judging performance will take longer.

In selecting funds, never forget that they are all run by business people who want to make money. Integrity is important to most managers, but, especially with new offerings, the sponsors may be promoters who sell the sizzle and neglect the steak.

Try to make a long-term commitment. Add savings regularly. Sell only when you really need the money, when your objectives change, or when you retire and shift into a withdrawal mode.

Concentrate on the fundamentals: the character of the sponsors, the record of management in achieving fairly consistent and rewarding returns in line with the objectives stated in the prospectus. Above all, do the results meet your specific goals?

## Study the record for the last ten years
This is long enough, usually, to show you performance in both up and down markets. Pay little heed to short-term performance, no matter how dramatic or how highly touted by your broker. Any fund manager can be lucky with one or two hot stocks for a short period of time, but what you want is consistency over the long haul. With stock funds, this means a better than average total return (income plus capital gains) in strong markets and a lower than average decline in down periods. With bond funds, which we'll talk about more later, it means a steady flow of income and a narrow price range.

The best funds are those that invest on the basis of quality and value and, over time, achieve returns averaging better than 10 percent annually. If you invest a single sum in such a fund, and reinvest the profits, over ten years it will nearly triple in value. If you invest the same sum every year, your investment will grow sixteen-fold in the same period of time. Remember the effect of compounding.

You can check the results of mutual funds in special sections put out by various business and financial publications. *Forbes* magazine ranks funds in both up and down markets. You may be surprised at how few funds continue to be rated A and AA.

## Discover how long large blocks of stock have been held
Were those ten thousand shares of IBM bought at 60 in 1981 or at 150 in 1985?

## How long were big-winning stocks held?
Were they purchased some months ago at a modest price, or at high cost just before the end of the last quarter, to make the report look good?

## What types of stocks are held?
If the fund concentrates more than 40 percent of its assets in big blue chips such as IBM and Merck, the managers are buying securities and reputation. A smart manager will hold such stocks but, except when they are at bargain prices, in limited quantities, because there will be other less famous firms whose selection requires special research and knowledge. That's what you are paying for!

## Do the managers use leverage to speculate?
Are they borrowing to trade, selling short, or dealing in options? All of these techniques can be risky. The profits can be welcome when the managers guess right, but the losses will be hard to recover when they guess wrong.

### How diversified are the portfolios?
With the exception of A-rated bonds or utility stocks, a fund should have no more than 10 percent of its holdings in any one company, and no more than 20 percent of its holdings in any one industry.

### Is the turnover rate more than 50 percent?
High activity means the managers made mistakes or are more interested in speculating than investing. Such transactions can be expensive.

### Is management stable?
A good measure is no significant changes in top executives (except by death or retirement) or in control during the last three years. Investing is a long-term commitment that requires uniform policies, experience, and patience.

Finally, insist on integrity in its fullest sense. Beware of promotional claims, such as an ad for a government bond fund that bore the headline "10.08%, 100% government guaranteed." The implication is that this yield is backed by Uncle Sam. In reality, that guarantee applies only to the redemption value and interest payments of the underlying securities, and not to the market value of the fund.

## CONSIDER BOND MUTUAL FUNDS
...

As we noted earlier, mutual funds can also be used to invest in virtually all types of bonds, mortgages, and debt issues. The funds offer the advantages of low cost and the opportunity to invest or withdraw small sums. Also, because mutual funds provide ownership of an investment pool rather than a single security, you are buying a ready-made portfolio that is diversified as to type and maturities of debt. Most important is the capability to reinvest earnings, which allows you to benefit from the magic of compounding.

There are two major types of bond funds.

## Unit Trusts

The proceeds of the original sale of shares are invested in a basket of bonds. No changes are made in the fund until, as a result of calls and redemptions, the assets drop to about 20 percent of the initial offering. At this point, the fund is closed out, and the assets are distributed to shareholders.

## Managed Funds

Professionals trade in anticipation of shifts in the cost of money. If they guess right, the fund will outperform the bond market. If they make a mistake, you can lose money.

To find a bond fund fitted to your assets and goals, read the prospectus and talk with your broker or salesman. Review the portfolio and ask the management company what percentage of the bonds carry a rating below A. Be wary if it turns out to be more than 20 percent!

# FIFTEEN

......................

# FOREIGN INVESTMENTS: BE CAUTIOUS

With the world becoming one huge market, there are increasing investment opportunities with quality corporations abroad. Concentrate on countries with stable economies, such as Great Britain, France, Switzerland, the Netherlands, and the Far East (Hong Kong, Singapore, Japan, and Indonesia).

In almost every case, whether you go with debt or equity, you should make long-term commitments. Over the short term, there are too many opportunities for temporarily unfavorable developments, such as currency devaluation or restrictive taxation. The key is *quality:* companies that are financially strong, profitable, growing, and well managed, and with ten years of audited annual reports.

Be wary of "opportunities" in formerly communist countries. There is no way to judge the competence of corporate management in a competitive market, If the foreign firm is tied in with a quality American company, the risk will be less. However, the rewards may also be limited because of management's long-term policies.

## With Debt

Find out about Eurobonds. These are denominated in a variety of currencies—dollar, yen, marks—or, to minimize exchange fluctuations, in European Currency Units. The ECU is a weighted average of the currencies of members of the European Economic Community. With Eurobonds there is no withholding tax on the interest.

Unless you have personal knowledge or are dealing with a brokerage or investment firm that has strong experience in overseas dealings, choose mutual funds. You will be buying diversification and some degree of selection expertise.

## With Equity

The most convenient choices are American Depositary Receipts (ADRs). These are negotiable receipts representing ownership of shares of a foreign corporation. They are issued by an American bank against securities held abroad, usually by a bank located in the country where the foreign corporation is headquartered. They are traded like stocks. A few are listed on the New York Stock Exchange; some on the American Stock Exchange, and most are traded over the counter.

Each ADR is a contract between the investor and the bank. The U.S. purchaser pays in dollars and receives dividends and interest in dollars. The bank handles all mechanical details, such as reports and stockholder voting.

To qualify for ADRs, the foreign firm must submit its financial statements to the Securities and Exchange Commission, so the investor can count on accurate (though not always complete or intelligible) information.

The market values of ADRs are subject to the same pressures as those on the underlying foreign stocks, and they also reflect the changing value of the U.S. dollar.

---

**FIGURE 15.1**

---

## Some ADRs Traded on American
## Stock Exchanges

| Company | Nation | Company | Nation |
|---|---|---|---|
| AEG Telefunken | Germany | Ericsson Telephone | Sweden |
| Amer. Israel Paper | Israel | Heineken | Netherlands |
| Anglo-American | So. Africa | Marks & Spencer | United Kingdom |
| Bowater Corp. | United Kingdom | Pirelli | Italy |
| Broken Hill | Australia | Royal Dutch | Netherlands |
| Canon | Japan | Tokyo Marine/ Fire | Japan |
| Deutsche Bank | Germany | Toyota Motor | Japan |

---

## Mutual Funds

These are available in three general types:

- *Global funds.* These funds make investments in any country, including the United States. They provide diversification and the opportunity to switch holdings between U.S. firms that are expanding within foreign markets and foreign companies when they are prospering to take advantage of changes in comparative economic conditions.
- *International funds.* Invest according to the future prospects of individual firms rather than national base or position in markets. Fund managers tend to move out of troubled countries and into those where prospects are bright.
- *Country-specific funds.* Invest in one country or a related group. The risks can be greater, but so are potentially higher returns, if the managers make the right choices.

Always check whether the fund is open or closed-end. With the former, the shares are purchased and redeemed at net asset value—the worth of the underlying securities. With the latter, the price is set by supply and demand in the marketplace, so that the shares often sell for less than the underlying value of the securities. This can represent an opportunity if investors become enthusiastic and boost the price of shares in the fund.

Here's a commonsense strategy: split your investment among two or three funds that have performed best over the last two years. Always limit your foreign holdings to 15 percent of your portfolio. It's difficult enough to make money with the securities of American companies, which are required to provide full information and whose fortunes are followed in the financial press. When you move abroad, where information is generally much more limited and your experience undoubtedly less, you are taking extra risks. And remember: successful investing always takes twice as long as you had anticipated.

# SIXTEEN

.................

# SPECIAL INVESTMENT TACTICS

There are scores of strategies and tactics touted by stock market gurus as "sure" routes to profits. In most cases, the sponsors make more money from the sales of their publications than the subscribers ever do from following their counsel. There are, however, a number of techniques that entail no special charges and can be rewarding for regular savings, such as those of pension plans.

## DOLLAR COST AVERAGING (DCA)
•••

With this formula plan, you invest a set sum of money at regular intervals, as with pension plan contributions. Then, each month or each quarter, you take this fixed sum of money and invest it in the stock of a *quality* company. Over time, your average cost per share will always be less than the average price of the stock. Reinvest all dividends to maximize your benefit from the effects of compounding. With this system, with a quality stock, your assets will grow steadily.

DCA takes patience and courage. You must have confidence in the future of the company whose shares you acquire, and you must be willing to keep investing during bear markets. Because you'll be putting the same amount of money into the stock each time you buy, you'll buy more shares during bear markets, when the stock price is down, than you do during bull markets, when the price is up. This lowers your average cost per share.

---

### FIGURE 16.1

## The Value of Dollar Cost Averaging

| Month | $100 per Month Cost Per Share | Shares Bought | Average Cost Per Share |
|---|---|---|---|
| | **During market upswing and fallback** | | |
| 1 | $13.45 | 7.435 | $13.45 |
| 2 | 13.89 | 7.199 | 13.67 |
| 3 | 14.27 | 7.008 | 13.86 |
| 4 | 14.66 | 6.821 | 14.05 |
| 5 | 14.22 | 7.032 | 14.09 |
| 6 | 13.74 | 7.278 | 14.03 |
| | **During market rise** | | |
| 7 | 14.01 | 7.138 | 14.02 |
| 8 | 14.55 | 6.873 | 14.19 |
| 9 | 14.86 | 6.729 | 14.17 |
| 10 | 15.52 | 6.443 | 14.29 |
| 11 | 15.60 | 6.410 | 14.40 |
| 12 | 15.92 | 6.281 | 14.52 |

The average cost per share is lower than current value in a rising market. As long as share value continues to increase, your average cost will always be lower than the current cost per share.

No system can guarantee that a fool will not lose his money in the stock market, but, with consistent investment under DCA, your assets will always be worth a lot more in time. Figure 16.1 shows what happens when you invest $100 a month. At the outset, with the stock at $13.45 a share, you acquire 7.435 shares; in the second month, when the price is up to $13.89, you buy 7.199 shares. By month six, with the market down, your average is *above* the current price of the stock, and you begin to doubt the system! However, you persevere, and by year's end you're glad you did. At this point you own 82.647 shares with an average cost of $14.52 —well below the current price of $15.92. (For the purposes of this illustration no commissions were charged, but, usually, these will be paid for by the dividends.)

With DCA, choose stocks of quality corporations that have a record of high profitability (earning 15 percent on equity) and whose shares keep moving up, but without great volatility (a ten-year high that is at least five times the low): General Electric, 71 vs. 11; General Mills, 90 vs. 10; or Sara Lee, 33 vs. 2½—all adjusted for stock splits.

## SYSTEMATIC PURCHASE PLANS
···

One way to execute a DCA plan is through a broker's systematic purchase plan, usually for a minimum investment of $25 per month. Fill out the application form, which commits you to a scheduled savings plan, list the name of the company whose shares you wish to purchase, and enclose a check for $25—or arrange for the money to be deducted from your money market account. If you're investing larger sums, you may want to split the money among two or three stocks.

## DIVIDEND REINVESTMENT
···

Many companies, primarily utilities, have plans that will automatically invest your dividends to purchase new shares of the company's stock. The commissions are low (averaging 1 percent plus a service charge to a maximum of $3.50) and you can with-draw all or part of the holdings at your convenience.

This tactic works particularly well with shares of mutual funds, where you buy diversification and can count on accurate reports for your income tax return—important because you are liable for income taxes on reinvested dividends except when the investments are held in tax-deferred pension plans or trusts.

# TACTICS FOR THE RETIRED
...

Many retirees worry about running out of money. This fear can be genuine but, in most cases, the problems will be limited and will only crimp life-style. This possibility can be the result of two factors:

## 1. Living too long

Actuarial-table life expectancies are averages but, under IRS rules, they set the timespan for payouts of pension plans. According to actuarial tables, a 65-year-old man is expected to live to age 80 and a same-age woman to 83.2. But the fastest growing age group is the over-85s. In Florida, between 1980 and 2020, these old-olds are projected to rise in number by 370 percent!

Worse, the actuaries have been wrong! According to the then-relied-on actuarial tables, almost all of the members of my Yale Class of 1931 are supposed to be dead. Yet, with an average age of 82, 30 percent are still alive, and we were well enough to raise more than $2.4 million at our sixtieth reunion!

## 2. Inflation

Even at an average annual rate of 4 percent, increases in the cost of living will cut purchase power by one third in ten years. There's not much the individual can do about inflation beyond smart shopping, careful consumption, and more do-it-yourself projects.

The effects of inflation and longevity generally start to create some financial pressure about fifteen years after retirement—roughly in the early eighties. Do not panic. There are a number of safe and conservative ways that you can create more income. You can sell property to your children, utilize special types of mortgages, buy tailored-to-need insurance policies (such as the Retirement Assurance policies that we discussed in Chapter 10), and write options on stock that you own.

With all of these possibilities, go slow, be sure you understand what will or may happen, consult experts, and make certain that your decisions are known to your heirs.

---

### FIGURE 16.2

---

### Writing Calls for Extra Income

September: Bought 300 shares XYZ @ 40 = $12,000
+ $150 costs = $12,150
Sold 3 March 40 calls @ 3¾ ($375) =
+ $1,125 − $50 costs =                        + 1,075
October/January dividends @ 50¢ share      +    300
                              Total income        $1,375
    This was deposited in Grandma's bank account.
March: XYZ stock at 42, so calls exercised: $12,000
− $150 costs = $11,850
Net loss of $300, leaving $11,850 to buy new share.

---

October: Bought 300 shares AHP @ 51 = $15,300
+ $160 costs = $15,460
Sold 3 April 50 calls @ 5 ($500) = $1,500
− $60 costs =                              $1,440
October/January/April dividends @ $2 share =    1,800
                    Deposited in bank account        + 3,240
April: AHP stock at 56, so shares called at 50.
$15,000 − $180 costs = $14,820      Loss of $640

---

**FIGURE 16.2 (continued)**

---

November: Bought 300 shares PBI @ $49½ = $14,850
                 + $170 costs = $15,020
                 Sold 3 May 50 calls @ 4½ ($450) = $1,350
                 − $50 costs =                                    $1,300
                 December/March dividends @ 70¢ share =        420
                                        to bank account    $1,720
May: PBI stock at 48 so kept stock and, two months later, when
its price rose to 49, sold new calls @ 3¼ ($325 each).

---

## Writing options on stock you own

A good way to create additional income safely. This technique
requires modest capital—an investment portfolio of $60,000 to
$100,000; the assistance of an experienced broker or investment
adviser, and an individual who is not overly concerned with leav-
ing a large estate and is willing to accept a modest reduction of
capital.

Properly executed, under a disciplined schedule, the writing
of options on stocks of quality companies is a low-risk endeavor.
For best results, do your research with books, pamphlets, and
adult education courses; paper-test the tactic for a month or two.

When you write (sell) options, you pocket a sure, immediate
profit rather than waiting for an uncertain, but potentially greater,
future gain. You are, in effect, borrowing (without interest) on
securities that you own.

There are two kinds of options: puts and calls. We're primarily interested in calls: the right to buy a specified number of shares
(usually 100) of a specified stock at a specified ("striking") price
before a specified expiration date, typically (but not always) three,
six, or nine months in the future. Puts are the opposite: the right
to sell the stock under similar terms.

Options on shares of more than 1,000 major corporations are
traded on stock exchanges. The quotations are available in major

financial publications and usually are listed at round figures, five points apart: 40–45–50, for example.

The cost of the option is called the premium. It varies with the duration of the contract, the type of the stock, corporate prospects, and the activity of the stock market. Premiums can range as high as 15 percent of the value of the underlying stock in a buoyant market. For instance, for a volatile stock, selling at 50 ($5,000 per one hundred shares), the premium for a call, at a strike price of 50 with a six-month expiration date, might be 7½ ($750 per one hundred shares). For shorter-term calls on a stable stock, the premium would be smaller—2 percent for those expiring in a month or so. A six-month call on such a stock might carry a 5 percent premium.

When you write a call on stock you own, the buyer pays you a premium because he thinks the stock price will rise more than the striking price plus the premium—and so he will make a profit. You, the seller, receive immediate income, but you may also have to sell your shares in the future, for less than they're worth at that time. However, if the market price of the stock price fails to exceed the striking price, the buyer will not exercise his option to buy, because there's no profit in it for him. You, the seller, keep the shares and can write new calls.

The best strategy is to write calls on three hundred shares of a well-rated company. With smaller units, the income will be reduced too much by commissions and fees.

With stocks priced at between $30 and $50 per share, the monthly investment for three hundred shares will be between $9,000 and $15,000. If you're planning on writing six-month calls every month, you'll need a total of between $54,000 and $90,000—enough money to buy six batches of three hundred shares. Remember: every call ties up a batch of shares for six months. Then you get to recycle the shares or, if they're sold, the proceeds.

Write on-the-money calls: at 40 when the stock is trading at 39. The premium will be high and the possibility of loss low.

## Case History

My mother (Dorcas's grandmother) was an eighty-four-year-old widow living in an Adult Congregate Living Facility (ACLF). Because of the costs of medicines and treatments, she needed an extra $750 per month. Her investment portfolio was worth about $70,000.

Working with a skilled broker, we adjusted the portfolio so that it contained three hundred shares of each of six stocks. We set an income goal of $9,000 per year. We planned to sell calls, with six-month expiration dates, on three hundred shares every month. Since calls are packaged in units of one hundred shares, we were writing three calls a month. See Figure 16.2 for how this program went. (The stock trade numbers have been simplified by assuming that we bought each batch of three hundred shares the same month we wrote the options.)

Over the year, Mrs. Hardy received total income, from premiums and dividends, of $11,025. After deductions for commissions and fees, the value of her portfolio was down about $1,000, but that affected only her estate, not the all-important income.

This strategy works best when the retiree is in a low tax bracket. In a strong market, you won't achieve the highest profits; in a poor market, you may have some paper losses.

# SEVENTEEN

# PUTTING IT ALL TOGETHER

Successful retirement portfolios are the result of an early start, discipline, insistence on quality, and intelligent diversification. Even with modest sums, you should plan your investments by categories: first, money market funds or certificates of deposit; then stocks, for growth or income as you prefer; next, debt issues. As a rule of thumb, plan for a minimum holding, in any one category, of $5,000—even if the regular investment is only $100! If you opt for mutual funds, use the same categories with a minimum commitment of $10,000 in each category. To build financial security, set your sights high—a minimum of $100,000, preferably $250,000, and, for peace of mind, $500,000.

The goal should be to accumulate assets that will be financially secure and will provide the income you need for as long as you and your ever-loving expect to live—not just actuarial life expectancy!

Start with life insurance actuarial tables and add or subtract years according to (1) personal health projections as indicated by your physician; (2) the longevity of your female ancestors; and, increasingly, (3) your efforts to foster good health by proper nutrition, exercise, and mental outlook.

## Example

At age 65, a man can expect to live 15 years, a woman, 18.2 years. At 70, the figures are 12.1 and 15. At 75, they are 9.6 and 12.1 respectively. Or to put the projections in terms of death years: At 65, a man can expect to live to be 80, a woman 83.2. At 70, 82.1 and 85; at 75, 84.6 and 87.1.

Next, be pessimistic and calculate the impact of inflation. For easy figuring, use ten, fifteen, and twenty years and an annual rate of increase of 4 percent. Look back to Figure 6.2 in Chapter 6, and you will see that the factors are 1.48, 1.80, and 2.19. Let's say you're retiring this year, and you expect your annual expenses to be about $30,000. Multiply that sum of money by the factors. To maintain your life-style, in ten years you will need an income of $44,400; in fifteen years you will need $54,000; and in twenty years you will need $65,700.

Before you cancel all plans for retirement, recheck your potential income. If you are both entitled to Social Security, you can hope for between $15,000 and $20,000 a year (probably less because of the taxation of Social Security benefits). And you will be able to draw principal from your investments while the balance continues to compound tax-deferred. Still, you will need a sizable nest egg of your own to count on a retirement that is free of money worries.

Figure 17.1 provides a frame of reference for both pension and personal investment portfolios. The percentages of the allocations will change with the availability of dollars and with temporary priorities (five to ten years) such as the costs of a new home, children's education, and health care. But these figures reflect the experience of professional planners. If your decisions get out of line for any period of time, even if the investments are highly profitable, review your choices and reallocate.

In investing, over the years of retirement savings, the goal should be to beat the averages: in bull markets, by 20 percent (for

## FIGURE 17.1

### Diversification for Investment Portfolios: Pension and Personal

| Age Investments | 25–40 Pension | 25–40 Personal | 41–55 Pension | 41–55 Personal | 56–70 Pension | 56–70 Personal | Retired |
|---|---|---|---|---|---|---|---|
| Money Markets/CDs | 5% | 5% | 5% | 5% | 5% | 5% | 10% |
| Bonds: straight | 5 | — | 10 | 10 | 20 | 15 | 25 |
| Bonds: zeros | 20 | — | 25 | — | 20 | 20 | 10 |
| Bonds: tax-exempts | — | — | — | 5 | — | 20 | 10 |
| Bonds: pass-throughs | — | — | — | — | — | — | 10 |
| Stocks: income | 20 | 10 | 20 | 15 | 25 | 10 | 20 |
| Stocks: growth | 50 | 70 | 40 | 55 | 30 | 45 | 25 |
| Speculations | — | 15 | — | 10 | — | 5 | — |

instance, an average annual rate of return of 12 percent, against 10 percent for the market as a whole); in bear markets, aim for a decline substantially less than that of the broad indicators.

Here's an explanation of the various investments:

## Money Markets/CDs
During your working years, keep an average of 5 percent of your money in this category, with greater sums in periods of economic uncertainty. After age seventy, boost the figure to 10 percent. Older people always seem more comfortable when they have ample ready cash for emergencies. Practically, it seems to me, you can keep less here and use credit cards to pay for emergency trips and unexpected expenses.

## Bonds: straight
Use these for income and peace of mind. The percentage should rise with age, from 5 percent for a new pension plan to 25 percent in retirement.

## Bonds: zero
Use these only in pension portfolios because of the income taxes on the imputed interest which is not received. Plan for purchases to mature after retirement.

## Bonds: tax-exempts
These are for your personal savings, with the amounts keyed to taxable income.

## Bonds: pass-throughs (such as Ginnie Maes)
These are most useful after retirement, when there is need for steady, generally rising income. Be cautious, as the life of these investments may be limited, especially in periods of declining interest rates, when homeowners will pay off their high-rate mortgages.

## Stocks: income

Here you need primarily shares of utilities, which keep boosting payouts. At all ages, with both types of savings, these stocks provide balance and assured income. Sell when the dividends falter.

## Stocks: growth

Here the maximum commitment for both personal and fiduciary funds should be when you are young, so you can benefit from the long-term appreciation of quality corporations. If there's a need for more income in retirement, start selling and shifting to income holdings.

## Speculations

These are not recommended, but, realistically, most folks at any age will dabble a bit. Never commit more than 15 percent of the portfolio, and then only when you're young and have time to recoup the losses. Unfortunately, the opposite usually happens: Yuppies spend so liberally that they save too little and then choose safety; older folks tend to strive to make one last try to make it big and, with few exceptions, lose their shirts.

# HOW TO SELECT FINANCIAL ADVISERS
•••

In the financial world, the right kind of counsel can help you attain your investment goals, keep you from making some mistakes, and, in time, teach you to be your own money manager. The selection is important because, usually, you get what you pay for.

When your assets are limited, there are two primary choices:

- Do it yourself by garnering information from financial publications—newpapers, magazines, statistical reports, market letters, and books.
- Buy shares of mutual funds, where all buy and sell decisions

are made for you by professionals who have access to information on the economy and securities.

When you have, or can soon anticipate, holdings of $200,000, an investment adviser can be worthwhile. With wise selection and sensible implementation, the costs of such service can be returned many times over, in peace of mind and dollars.

These professional money managers should be considered as financial physicians who help to heal ailing investments, prescribe a regimen to nurture your wealth, and enhance your fiscal fitness through periodic checkups and profitable money management. There are two types:

- Those who charge for information, directly or through printed media, and make recommendations that you can accept, modify, or reject.
- Those who manage your money for a fee, usually based on the value of your assets—typically 1 percent but less with larger accounts.

While rewarding returns can be important, most older investors look for peace of mind and convenience. Here's a checklist for selecting a financial adviser:

## Comfort
Pick someone with whom you (and your spouse) feel at ease, whose advice you are willing to follow or (with discretionary accounts) accept. A good adviser operates in a professional manner, with integrity, intelligence, prudence, and adherence to your personal goals.

## Reputation
Look at how long the organization has been in existence, at the experience of top officers. Listen to the opinions of clients who you know and respect.

The reputation should be professional, not personal. Look for proven performance, not images of success such as Gucci shoes, Bond Street clothes, and membership in exclusive clubs.

## Results
Look at the track record (preferably audited) over the last ten years. This is normally a long enough period to cover performance in both bull and bear markets. For stocks, the average annual total return (income plus appreciation) should be significantly better than the performance of the Standard & Poor's 500 Stock Composite. With bonds, compare to the AA Bond Average.

Beating these norms may sound easy, but only 20 percent of all professionals have long-term records better than the overall market.

## Types of Clients
A substantial number of clients should be individuals with goals and assets similar to yours. This may require a shift over the years: from aggressive managers when you're young enough to recoup losses, to conservators when you're getting ready for retirement and need ample income and minimal loss of capital.

To check, ask for typical portfolios over the years. Then, see the decisions made in different types of markets for different types of clients.

## Services
Who will handle your account—a seasoned veteran or a young assistant under qualified direction? What reports will you receive? How will additions and withdrawals be handled? At what cost?

From friends and other clients, find out the efficiency of the organization. Is extra cash moved quickly into money market funds? Are checks sent promptly? Are questions answered fully and quickly?

## Strategy and Tactics
Is the philosophy compatible with yours? What is the source of research? Is the turnover rate in investments low? It shouldn't be

more than 20 percent, except in critical periods or when you're speculating with high activity, commissions can cut your profits. And can also be a sign that mistakes have been made.

Finally, be careful about relying too much on your broker for investment advice. He/she can be helpful in many ways, obtaining information, keeping you advised of the tax and other legal implications of your investing, and commenting on your decisions. But remember, a broker is a salesperson.

While they're working, most people can afford to take some investment risks. In retirement, though, losses can be damaging and distressing. *Any investment that seems too good to be true probably is.* Find out the rationale for all "special opportunities" and, probably, start looking for a new adviser.

## THE SUCCESSFUL INVESTOR
...

To be a successful investor:

### Diversify (but not too much)
Spread the risk, catch special opportunities, and strive for a steady rate of return and appreciation. With less than $100,000, you should own ten issues, preferably in five groups. With a portfolio between $100,000 and $1 million, you should have not more than twenty issues, perhaps three debt holdings and seventeen equities. No one holding should represent more than 10 percent of total funds at cost or 15 percent at market value. In down periods, shift the portfolio so that 50 percent or more is in debt holdings.

### Set targets
When you buy a stock, set the price at which you are going to sell it—usually 25 to 50 percent above the purchase price. When the stock approaches the target level, get ready to sell unless you can *logically* anticipate a similar gain in the near future.

## Never be in a hurry to spend your money

Logic is a rarity with many folks who handle their own funds. Reason and research are overcome by ego, impatience, and greed. Most folks like to boast of fast, super profits, but they seldom admit their more frequent (and usually costlier) failures. Before you make any financial commitment, consider what *could* happen if you are wrong about the economy or the targeted security.

Keep your money in a money market account until you feel comfortable. You don't want to worry about what you might have to confess to your spouse!

## Be patient

Usually a stock will flex its muscles—up a little, down a little, up a little more—before taking off. Wait for confirmation of your projections sparked by higher quarterly earnings, an optimistic research report, or a favorable news story. Another good indicator is institutional interest as indicated by heavier trading volume.

## Periodically review your portfolios

See that they stay in balance and in tune with the future that you're projecting. Too often, when you pick a stock that proves to be a winner, you keep adding shares—and suddenly 30 percent of your savings is concentrated in one stock. That's too much for fiduciary funds.

## Insist on quality

Quality investments will always be worth more in the future—unless the company ceases to deserve a quality rating.

## Recognize that it is more important to avoid losses than to achieve gains

For every 20 percent loss, to break even, the gain must be 25 percent. For an equal bounce-back from a 20 percent loss, you need to go up 50 percent from the trough. Thus, if the stock drops from 100 to 80 (a 20 percent loss), it has to move back to 100 (a

25 percent increase) to erase the loss; to 120 to achieve the originally projected 50 percent profit.

## Make your own projections as to the probable future of the security

Most research reports will be overly optimistic, as they are designed to help brokers make sales and earn commissions. Here's an example of how you can make your calculations:

In late 1981, Connie, a middle-aged office manager, decided she liked the products of Mythical Corporation (MC). She checked and found that the firm was rated A +, had reported an average annual return on equity of more than 15 percent for the last seven years, and had paid ever-higher dividends. She was also impressed with an optimistic research report, which projected that earnings would increase by 12 percent for the next three years.

Figure 17.2 shows her calculations. She conservatively estimates a 10 percent annual increase in profits: per share earnings to rise from $3.18 in 1982 to $6.18 in 1989. Connie assumes that the stock will consistently trade at eleven times earnings (this figure is the price/earnings of P/E ratio in the newspaper's stock tables). She therefore projects that, in 1989, the stock will be selling at 68—almost double its current 35.

---

### FIGURE 17.2

### How to Project the Future Value of a Quality Stock

Mythical Corporation

Projections of annual gains in profits of 10% and a market value of 11 times earnings (below the average for recent years).

| Year | Per Share Earning | | Range of Stock Price | |
|------|:---:|:---:|:---:|:---:|
| | Projected | Actual | Projected | Actual |
| 1982 |  | $3.18 | 35 | 48–34 |
| 1983 | $3.50 | 3.60 | 38 | 54–42 |

| 1984 | 3.85 | 4.00 | 42 | 56–46 |
| 1985 | 4.23 | 4.40 | 46 | 66–50 |
| 1986 | 4.65 | 4.70 | 51 | 94–62 |
| 1987 | 5.11 | 5.18 | 56 | 84–70 |
| 1988 | 5.62 | 5.74 | 61 | 110–80 |
| 1989 | 6.18 | 6.38 | 68 | 110–94 |
| 1990 * | | 3.65 | | 52 |

* Stock split 2–1 in 1990.

The real results were even more rewarding. The stock price rose steadily to 110 in 1990, when there was a two-for-one split. The original shares, bought for $3,500, became two hundred shares worth more than $10,000. Add some $2,000 in dividends and the total increase in value was $12,000, more than triple the original investment. That's building retirement security!

## Calculate the reward/risk ratio before making a commitment

This is a handy way to determine whether the potential reward, from a higher stock price, is greater than the possible loss due to a mistake or unfavorable conditions. For our example, let's use Connie and Mythical Corporation again.

When Connie reviewed MC, it was trading at 35 and had a P/E ratio of 11. Using a five-year frame, Connie projected that, on the upside, the stock could reach 56. (This is the same calculation she did before, using a projected 10 percent annual increase in profits and a P/E ratio of 11.) On the downside, Connie estimated that the stock would go no lower than the low of 25 that it had experienced in 1978.

Using these figures, Connie calculated potential reward and risk. The reward was 21 points up (35 to 56). The risk was ten points down (35 to 25). The reward/risk ratio was therefore 2.1 (21 divided by 10). Any ratio above 1.0 is favorable so, at the time, MC was a buy.

When MC reached 100, the low figure was 50 (in 1985) and the projected high, 110; now the reward was 10 and the risk 50: an R/R ratio of 0.2. It was time to consider selling but, since a two-for-one stock split had been announced and a price peak usually follows such news, Connie held until the stock hit 110, sold out at a welcome profit, and put her money in a bond fund.

## One final word

For profitable investing, insist on quality, look for value, and be patient!

# EPILOGUE

....................

Changes in the financing of retirement are inevitable: with Social Security, because there will not be enough money to pay the promised benefits; with retirement plans, because of the pressure to encourage more rewarding methods of savings and to expand personal responsibilities.

Social Security's basic commitments will be met but its financing and payments are so much a part of the national economy that the system's difficulties will have a tremendous impact on our future.

The timing and format of revisions that will be hammered out in Congress will, as always, be compromises. Possibly, there will be a reduction or revision of benefits through fewer or reduced COLAs; probably, an ever-higher eligibility age; and certainly, increased taxes on earnings or benefits or both. Most significant will be legislation to place greater emphasis on individual savings.

These changes will be achieved slowly and reluctantly because of the nature of our political process. Within Congress, the revisions will be hampered by the views of some members who will continue to bottle up what most people see as logical proposals. Noisy interest groups which do not reflect the views of the majority of their membership as well as rhetoric by candidates who seek headlines above solutions will complicate the controversial discussions. The final decisions will antagonize those seniors who view all benefits as rights and foster among younger persons even greater disillusionment with the role and responsibilities of government. However, most people will recognize that changes are essential and overdue.

To achieve viable solutions, there must be a better understanding of the role of all American retirement systems and the development of better methods to encourage individuals to balance end-of-life leisure with while-working financial contributions.

There's nothing wrong in government guaranteeing old-age security through a social insurance structure, but it's time that these subsidies are recognized and controlled in a more equitable manner. Those elderly who want to work should not be penalized, nor should the Social Security system continue to provide incentive for early retirement. We should recognize that Social Security, as now constituted, is a public transfer program which makes possible basic retirement for some and joyous leisure for upper-income retirees.

Fortunately, America can count on new leadership which will be concerned, innovative, and aggressive. These will be the baby boomers with their affluence, enthusiasm, optimism, and realistic approach to problems. As proven with the computer revolution, these "youngsters" are willing to experiment, to welcome change, and to seek solutions rather than accept the status quo. They enjoy change and are already beginning to recognize that Social Insecurity is their problem. We are confident that they can, and will, find solutions.

The crisis is coming fast—in the lifetime of a few already retired and of almost all those now under age 55. The stakes are high—trillions of dollars. Most important, there will be a change in focus from significant dependence on government retirement financing

(50 percent of retirement income) to greater personal responsibility through personal savings and pension plans.

Social Insecurity will be one of the most important subjects for the United States in the next decade. That's why everyone who has read this book should become involved in helping to achieve an effective solution. Explain the dire facts to neighbors and peers, to children and grandchildren. Encourage private business to develop new plans for savings, investment, and insurance. Become involved in concerned national organizations and help your elected representatives to act decisively and *soon*.

What you do, or do not do, about Social Security, as well as your individual portfolio, will make the difference between fear and joy in your later years. If you vote for "joy," start campaigning now.

# INDEX

. . . . . . . . . . . .

Treasury bills, 126
Treasury bonds, special-issue
 investment of Social
 Security tax revenues in, 18,
 21–22, 47
 redeeming, 18, 22, 47
Treasury notes, 126
trust funds, 4, 6, 17, 21
12(b)-1 fees, 134
two-career families, 29

Ullman, Rep. Al, 13
unit trusts, 138
U.S. Chamber of Commerce, 30,
 32
U.S. Congress
 and power of elderly lobby,
 15–17, 36
 proposals in, 42–50
 recommendations for, xv, 57–
 58, 60, 61, 63–64, 65
U.S. Department of Health and
 Human Services, xix, xx
U.S. Savings Bonds, 126
U.S. Social Security
 Administration (SSA), xx,
 52
U.S. Treasury bills, 126
U.S. Treasury notes, 126

wage indexing, 53–54
wage rates, relative to prices, 11,
 13
wage-replacement ratio, 24, 30–
 31
*Wall Street Journal,* 34, 44–45
wealth transfer
 in early years of Social
 Security, 10–11
 Social Security as, 25–26
 Social Security becomes, 6
Williams, Walter, 30
women
 early retirement for, xxiv
 fertility rate of, 28–29
 in two-career families, 29–30
workers
 low-income, 23–24, 31, 41
 percent covered by Social
 Security, 3, 11
 ratio of retirees to, 12, 23, 39
 wage-replacement ratio of, 24,
 30–31
writing of options, 147–50

Yankelovich, Skelly and White,
 30

zero coupon bonds, 127–28

C. COLBURN HARDY is nationally recognized for his writing and activities in the financial and aging fields. He has written twenty-six books on investments, money management, and retirement, and has served on national and state committees including the Florida Pepper Commission on Aging.

DORCAS R. HARDY was Commissioner of Social Security and Assistant Secretary of Health and Human Services under Presidents Reagan and Bush. She has hosted a television show on Financial News Network and is now a consultant to major corporations and associations on legislation, aging policies, and retirement planning.